Jim Thompson was ordained after working as an accountant; he was Chaplain at Ripon College, Cuddesdon, Rector of Thamesmead, Bishop of Stepney, and Bishop of Bath and Wells. He is a well-known broadcaster and was shortlisted for a Sony Broadcasting Award for his 'Thought for the Day' on 12 September 2001, following the terrorist attacks in the USA.

To Sally

GOOD MORNING!

A Decade of
Thoughts for the Day

Bishop Jim Thompson

Published in Great Britain in 2003 by
Society for Promoting Christian Knowledge
Holy Trinity Church
Marylebone Road
London NW1 4DU

British Library Cataloguing-in-Publication Data
A catalogue record for this book is available from the British Library

1 3 5 7 9 10 8 6 4 2

ISBN 0-281-05498-3

Typeset by Kenneth Burnley, Wirral, Cheshire
Printed in Great Britain by
Antony Rowe, Chippenham, Wiltshire

Contents

Contents

Contents

Foreword

You really need to *watch* Jim broadcasting his 'Thought for the Day' to appreciate it fully. His brow furrows, his whole body tenses, his hands clench. And then, when he has finished, he sits there for a moment, lost in himself. I suspect he is wondering whether it was good enough, whether he has used his two and three quarter minutes wisely and well. He need have no doubts.

Jim Thompson has none of the pomposity and self-regard that afflict some other men who have risen to such great heights in the Church of England. He is a modest man whose decency shines through in every word he utters. We presenters tend, rather unkindly, to rank our 'thinkers'. Those who end up at the bottom of the list are the ones who often use their few minutes to spout pious platitudes, create spurious links between the spiritual and the temporal, and to imply that they, and they alone, have all the answers. Jim does none of that. He is a man of deep faith, but he has come to that faith only after some long and difficult struggles; he knows what it is like to doubt – which is one of the reasons why his 'Thoughts' are never self-satisfied or smug, neither sentimental nor sanctimonious. He does not seek to present his God in pretty tissue paper tied up with a velvet bow.

Jim addresses real issues – not just life and death, but the cruelty, for instance, that can accompany both. He tells us, in one 'Thought', of the beautiful kingfisher flashing past his window, diving into the water to catch a fish – and then beating the fish to death. The images and the contrast work perfectly to demonstrate our role in God's creation.

Jim Thompson is a sixty-six-year-old retired bishop who has retained his sense of wonder and his curiosity and has all the delight in debate and argument of a bright young student. I hope he does many, many more 'Thoughts' – not just because they can lift the programme on a dull day, but because I would miss our occasional arguments. As a devout sceptic (to steal a Radio 4 title) I envy Jim his faith. As a journalist I admire his writing, his imagination and his sense of humour. As a human being, I admire his integrity. And you get it all in 'Thought for the Day' – in less than three minutes. No mean feat, that.

JOHN HUMPHRYS, *Today*, BBC Radio 4

Introduction

On 17 December 1991 I went, in the early morning of a dreary wet day, to Bath, to do my first Somerset-based 'Thought for the Day'. When I arrived at the studio it was locked. We waited and waited. At about 7.40 I realized we were not going to get in, and went to a telephone box and phoned my wife, Sally. It was now 7.45, and she dashed round the unfamiliar filing system trying to find the number of the *Today* studio. Meanwhile, back at the phone box, a BT operative had arrived to clean it and was getting frustrated both because he could not get access and also because the passing traffic kept throwing up mud. At 7.50 the phone rang and a voice said, 'Bishop Thompson, we're putting you through to the studio.' Brian Redhead, on air, said, 'Good morning, Jim – where are you?' 'I'm in a phone box.' 'What's that noise?' 'It's the buses and lorries going past,' I replied. Then Brian said, 'And what have you got for us this morning?' And I replied, 'I am talking about the impact of moving into a beautiful new environment . . .' The 'Thought' itself (page 1) was published in most of the daily papers and thousands of people have said to me since that they remember especially the 'Thought' from the phone box. Perhaps it was the vulnerability which was communicated.

Just before this 'Thought', I was appointed Bishop of Bath and Wells. It was a huge step for us to move from the London Boroughs of Tower Hamlets, Hackney and Islington, to the beautiful county of Somerset. Our new home was the historical and outstandingly lovely thirteenth-century Bishop's Palace in Wells. We were going to live surrounded by twenty-foot-high walls, and a freshwater moat next to the Cathedral and Market Square. Comments varied between ' What does he know about rural affairs?', 'Stepney! Can anything good come out of Stepney?' and, from the Stepney end, 'I can't believe you're leaving us' and 'He's done very well for himself!'

I am thankful to God and the people of Somerset that we have been happy there, and I have been honoured to be their Bishop. It has been a great privilege and joy to be closely associated with rural life and the farming community, as well as towns and cities. We had links with Somerset, first through holidays since childhood, and then through our own cottage since 1980. Now in retirement, we live on Exmoor, which had been a long-term dream.

When I was appointed to the job I was aware of tensions between many rural and urban people in the UK, and decided that I would try to work for better mutual understanding. Little did I anticipate BSE, 'right to roam', foot and mouth, and the pervasive hunting debate. Living as we do now on Exmoor, I already realize how fundamental are the differences in attitude, especially in relation to the natural world. So often urban people seem to be anaesthetized to the harshness of nature itself, and confused about the role of the human race in the ecological balance by which it develops. Having struggled for many years to encourage the growth of community spirit in the new town of Thamesmead, and in East London where so much sense of belonging had been undermined by bombing and 'planning', where so many familiar landmarks and personal links had been removed, I relished the smaller communities, where people knew each other, and felt in a sense re-humanized.

At the same time, I began to see how much rural people have to learn from urban people, and how intimately they depend upon the towns and cities, not just as customers, but also for cultural variety and support services. It is plainly absurd and prejudicial to our national well-being that such mutual ignorance and animosity exist. Obviously this tension can be overstated, and thankfully there are many people who have experience of both and can act as a bridge, but much education is still needed. In the past ten years these matters have engaged much of my time and take shape in this book.

But these 'Thoughts', like all the 'Thoughts', are not just about our own current experience but rather have to encompass a wide variety of issues. The world's news is the scope of the *Today* programme. Even questions about the universe are tackled. I have become more and more fascinated by the New Physics and especially the implications of the Big Bang and the Creation, of the extraordinary ecological balance of the earth and its mostly secure place in the solar system. Since my university days the stale old tape of science and religion inevitably being in conflict with each other is worn out, and thankfully discarded by many thinking theologians and scientists. The refreshing understanding of the Bible within its context and the frank recognition that it is not science nor is it always history, but often legend and meaning derived from the journey of faith, have helped theologians to look at science with a more open mind, not feeling they have to fit reality into a verbally inerrant box. This theologically open mind has met up with a greater humility in science and the recognition that the questions remain even when we have explored the universe and the earth at the micro and macro level. I have a strong conviction that the Christian faith has to face reality and go on searching for the truth, and not be scared, because where the truth takes us, there we shall find God ahead of us.

As we know, conflict, disaster and suffering are the stuff of the daily news. It's almost possible to become immune from thinking about such things. The starving children, the refugees and victims of war, the train, road and rail crashes, and above all for me, 11 September 2001. They all present the person doing 'Thought for the Day' with what appear to be unanswerable questions. When you consider the nature of the earth and its environment, death, risk and pain are part of the reality. There is a frightening ambiguity about the Creation itself. Water, fire, rocks, seas and winds all make a fundamental contribution to the possibility and the context of human freedom. Yet all of them possess the capacity to kill if we are in the wrong place at the wrong time. Although I find it difficult to conceive the purpose of dinosaurs being wiped out by a meteor, I do accept the awful risk of life itself.

But far more difficult is the constant assault of human evil – our inhumanity to each other, the wickedness and amorality of much human exchange. When we are faced with the task of expressing some hope, I believe we are thrust back on to the love of God in the human story. Based upon my own direct personal experience of the steadfast mercy of God, I try to express that hope without being naïve or presenting Jesus Christ as some simplistic solution. What we can say seems to rely on having some understanding of the human proneness to sin, but at the same time having the forgiving life and teaching of Christ to flicker some light into despairing dark places.

As for 11 September 2001, I was in my study preparing to induct the new Rector of Bath Abbey later that evening. My wife came in and told me that a disaster had happened in New York. I went through to watch the television and saw the horror unfolding. Should we postpone the service at the Abbey?

No, we should use the opportunity for prayer. All those people were coming. We had a meditation to start with and then began the service.

Only a few minutes before we left for Bath, the phone rang and the producer of 'Thought for the Day' asked me to stand by to broadcast in the morning. It wasn't certain, because the *Today* programme was exploring the possibility of an American doing it from New York. We got home at 10 p.m. and it was confirmed that I would do it. Somehow the whole of my energy and imagination had 'gone down' and I sat at the table trying to think what I could possibly say. The 'Thought' itself (page 119) describes what happened and I finished writing at 1 a.m. What I had to say seemed so totally inadequate, but the 'Thought' was repeated on *Pick of the Week* and was later nominated for a Sony award by the BBC. As always, what I tried to offer was empathy with the listeners and the attempt to be honest about the struggle going on.

Many of the subjects tackled are in the broad sense political. There have been politicians who have said that the bishops should not intervene in politics. Thankfully this incredible concept has fallen from favour in more recent years. It is not our task on 'Thought for the Day' to be party political. If others see what we are saying as party politics, when we are trying to describe reality in our society, or give ethical reflections or express policy, so be it. Faith and the Christian Gospel have huge political implications, and politicians do not own them. Because 'Thought' does not have immediate response, it is in a way protected time. The *Today* programme always tries to ensure that there is a balanced presentation of the issues, and this means that in our contributions we have to exert a discipline to avoid the misuse of this privileged position. The life, death and resurrection of Jesus Christ have political implication, and it is often through his own words that his vision can transcend the language of the political debate.

There is also a risk in publishing ten years of 'Thoughts', because with hindsight it may become apparent that I was wrong in my interpretation of what happened, or what later developed. An event like 11 September 2001 had to be reacted to immediately. It's not just a journalistic report of the event, but rather a personal attempt to understand, to give some hope, and, if possible, to look to the future. In a way it is a pastoral response to the suffering and the fears of many people. There is also an element of prophecy. So much of this can be proved wrong by events. I even had one occasion when I only had to wait a few minutes for the news to tweak what I had said.

In this selection, I have let the chosen 'Thoughts' stand as they were uttered, and trust the readers to make their own critique.

I hope they might do this with a little compassion! Prophecy is difficult in both its biblical senses, i.e. foretelling the future, and speaking for God. Both these aims make it clear that on this road there are many potholes.

The most demanding side of 'Thought for the Day' is the chance to articulate the presence of God in the daily news: not only God in a general sense, but the God and Father of Jesus Christ. I have been blessed by many signs of God in people of other faiths and I continue to learn much from them, but it was God identified in Jesus who turned my life round, and who has sustained, inspired and kept on forgiving and washing my soul. Although I long to communicate with every listener, whether atheist or agnostic, and those whom Schleiermacher called 'Cultured Despisers', my hope is that Christ will be made known to someone somewhere, or some encouragement given to those who are already searching and finding.

Some of the most frustrating times are when I long to talk about God in a context, which is then considered not to be newsworthy. It is a hard discipline. There are so many people who have written off faith as infantile, archaic or irrelevant. Indeed, the media often talk as if it is already gone. I notice the favourite phrase used to describe the Church is 'terminal decline', yet neither here in the UK nor around the world does that seem true, and it is certainly an insult to all those faithful people who still try to model their lives on the way of Christ. Day by day, I meet and share worship with thousands of people for whom faith has become more real than it was, who believe God's truth endures for ever. I do not know whether to get angry about this or to work harder out of pity for their arrogance. It is not just Christianity which bears this burden, but it is a costly mistake round the world that so little attempt is made to understand the religious dimensions of the national and international issues facing us. For instance, to try to produce solutions in Israel/ Palestine, or in Northern Ireland, or in Asia or Africa, without an imaginative and informed grasp of the religions of those involved, is patronizing in the extreme.

'Thought for the Day' plunges right into the deep end of the soul, where human beings are joined to God. To lose the sense of the sacred, and not to feel any awe or joy of the Holy, is to experience an absence and emptiness which can seriously affect our own wholeness. Faith is not dead as long as it continues to light up so many of the lives of those who have turned towards God. I still believe that every human being has a receiver which can be tuned into the divine. I know this can and does happen as people are driving to work, having a bath, or milking the cows.

I hope these 'Thoughts' will be of use. Perhaps they may stir up the sense of God within. Perhaps they may offer ideas for morning assembly in schools, or suggest discussion, or give a new angle on personal lives. For me, they have been part of a struggle to speak truly, and communicate the thrill of my life.

May I now thank all those who have helped me to sustain 'Thoughts' through nearly twenty-five years. Above all, thanks to my wife Sally who patiently listens to the fifth and sixth drafts, who makes important links, speaks English, has ideas when I am bereft, and suffers the disturbed nights which are often a precursor to the 'good morning' moment. Thank you also to my PA, Mary Masters, and my Chaplains in these ten years, Geoffrey Marlowe and then Martin Wright, who have constantly prayed with me and tried to keep me on the straight and narrow. A special word of gratitude to my secretary Penny Ritchie who typed all the 'Thoughts' and sent out many copies to people requesting another read.

I am very grateful to Eddy Lynch for all our early morning journeys over the Mendips to the Bath and Bristol studios. Thank you also to the team of producers who dare to say 'No' when I have sweated hard and long on a text, and who have nearly always been right. They have been wonderfully patient. Last but not least, thanks to Ruth McCurry who edited much of the book and on behalf of SPCK saw it through into production.

THE TELEPHONE BOX

17 December 1991

One of the arguments between Church and State in the last ten years has been about the impact of our environment on our moral behaviour. Our recent move from Stepney to Wells has made us think of this from a new angle as we have experienced a sort of environmental shock. Our dog thinks he's ascended to heaven! In East London our morning walk took us along the canal, which could be beautiful, but was nearly always marred by reminders of the tough old world around us. The pile of sacks and plastic bags which turned out to be a man sleeping rough . . . the obscene graffiti signalling that anti-Semitism and fascism are not dead . . . the rubbish thrown in the canal, redeemed once by the sight of five yellow ducklings riding royally downstream on a sheet of polystyrene. And then those characters in need of care from the community – the mentally sick or people who just can't cope; and in the background the dominating tower blocks.

Now our walk takes us through a sort of earthly paradise – round the moat where the kingfishers fly, out across the fields and through the woods; and above all, as we return home, there is the cathedral in all its perfection commanding the scene, suggesting not only the beauty of worship, but a sort of permanence in its ancient walls bathed by nearly a thousand years of prayer. In a hectic life, I find this new environment restoring me, reminding me of the wonder of God, giving my body space to catch up with my mind. It goes deep inside. The impact, or perhaps I should say the comfort, is profound.

I think of my many friends who live in East London – but especially those on the run-down estates, on the twelfth floor of a neglected tower block, where the lifts don't work, where overflowing pipes are left for months, where they have four locks on their front door, and where the night fear is so great they daren't go out after dark.

These conditions dishearten people, drain their energy and undermine their hope. Even so, there are many who overcome them and become saints and never let the impotence erode their spirit or their goodness. Environment is only one factor in the making of lives, and not even the most important. We have all known good people who have been brought up in poverty, and wicked people who have come from beautiful surroundings, but I have to say that one should never underestimate the impact on the soul of the place in which we live. Praise God at Christmas we are reminded that the gospel star shone over a stable where the baby lay, to demonstrate for all time that there is nothing in squalor or homelessness or poverty which can separate us from the love of God.

Note. This was my first 'Thought' as Bishop of Bath and Wells. The morning was wet and grey. No one came to open the studio, hence I used the telephone box (see page ix).

EUROPEAN FAITH?

18 December 1991

As politicians try to construct a new Europe, people have been afraid we shall lose our identity as a nation – our country! But almost nothing appears to have been said about another fear that we shall lose our God. It angers me that in all the hype about Maastricht, almost nothing was reported about the religious dimension. Yet to ignore it is to fly in the face of the past and indeed the present. It's not enough to talk finance and politics and ignore the faith factor. We can't begin to understand Northern Ireland, or the hatred between Serbs and Croats, or the tension between Greece and Turkey, or the break-up of the Soviet bloc, without taking into account the religious elements. Not only the conflicts between Christians, but between Christians and Muslims, Muslims and Jews, and so on. It remains a great indictment of religion that it has so often nourished intolerance, violence and war. We seem to be at a terrifying turning point, when we learn a new way or face disaster. The world cannot afford more crusades, fundamentalism and religious imperialism.

The difficulties are immense and it might be tempting to use the reconstruction of Europe to recreate old religious boundaries and within them try to impose a uniform religious identity. But wherever that's done, persecutions of minorities follow. We are a pluralist society, and Europe will be a pluralist Europe.

It seems to be a feature of the United Kingdom that the majority claim to be Christians, but only a relatively small percentage take their faith seriously – even though we still call ourselves a Christian country. This makes people nervous, even those who subscribe to other faiths. So from this position of weakness Christians are sometimes tempted to man the barricades and deny or denigrate any other vision of God. But this is religion in its fearful, negative and even aggressive mode.

So I believe each of us needs to learn to value our faith more highly, go deeper into it, not take it for granted. In this way we find security in what we believe, and a great confidence in God, and there's less need for aggression. Then perhaps Christians could realistically offer the wonder of Christ as the triumph of love and faith over fear. We have to discover real dialogue and understanding here. Perhaps then we could offer that as our particular pluralist contribution to the construction of a new Europe. We would be singing the song of the angels in our carol:

> All glory be to God on high
> And to the earth be peace.
> Goodwill henceforth from heaven to men
> Begin and never cease.

JESUS CHRISTMAS

19 December 1991

There is a true story of a woman who went into a wine shop. When her turn came to be served she was in such a state of fluster she couldn't remember what she'd come in for. In her anguish she said, 'Whoever invented Christmas should be shot!' to which the wine merchant replied, 'Well he wasn't shot exactly.'

But did Jesus invent Christmas? His birth was meant to be the centre of the celebration, but I suppose it was the Church which invented it. I wonder what Christ thinks of our Christmas now? What would be his list of dos and don'ts?

Here's my list from what we know of him:

- Don't get into rows, and if you're already in one, cease hostilities – like the soldiers in the First World War. Come out of your trenches and play football.
- Don't eat or drink to excess. 'Enough' is just as much fun, and the following morning will be much more life affirming. The food tastes better when you thank God for it, and the cook and those who provided it, and you remember those in need.
- Don't make Christmas such a complicated, carefully negotiated, burdened occasion that your home becomes a militarized zone – and a law by which you are oppressed as its slaves.

On the other hand, there are the dos:

- Do enjoy the children – give time to their innocent wonder, which Jesus said was a signpost to the Kingdom of Heaven, and try to prevent them becoming greedy, selfish little beasts.
- Do some act of love for those who are alone, or in prison, or

homeless, or hungry – or at least give generously and pray! And if you're one of those reliving grief, feeling alone, in prison, in hospital, or far from home – cultivate the presence of Christ. He is Emmanuel – God with us.

- Do make time for the love of God – go to midnight Mass if you're a Christian or a seeker, make some quiet time to let his healing, integrating grace fill your heart, and worship the Lord your God and his Son with carols and prayers and tell the old, old story. Reflect for a moment on your creator, Father of the universe and the generous, wonderful gift of his Son.

- Do celebrate and have fun and laugh until the tears roll down your face, and hug each other and look at photographs from the old box in the attic and sing some songs and play some undignified games, or be exalted by beautiful music or great drama or dancing, or whatever gives you a sense of abundant life – and then finish with a thought of Heaven. There they have the best feast of all.

I think we all invent our own Christmas each year by the way we spend it – and I hope yours will be a wonderful invention.

CARE IN THE COMMUNITY?

20 February 1992

After Terry Waite's moving return to the General Synod yesterday, we went on to debate the care of the mentally ill. It was not surprising how often Terry's words, carved out of his experience of isolation through years spent alone in a dark cell, were reflected in the debate. He spoke to all suffering people and said how much the words of scripture that the light would never be overcome by the darkness had meant to him. Members of the Synod spoke of personal experiences, whether of themselves or friends or relatives, who were afflicted with mental illness, and their isolation was a common theme.

There was a mental hospital near our home, and a little lady carrying plastic bags, wearing ill-fitting shoes and old clothes used to walk every day from the hospital to a squat, and she would stand for hours looking out of the upstairs window. This happened for two years. Then the property was bought, and the squat was emptied. The builders moved in. Still she came every day and walked up to the third floor and stared through the window, although it had gone and was replaced by scaffolding. Eventually the building works were finished and the house was occupied and I don't know what happened to her. I didn't know how to do anything to help her and thought thankfully of the work our Chaplain was doing in the hospital. More and more people like her are now having to live and survive out in the community.

In our Synod debate, we urged the government to go on to implement the community care programme, but we also called on the Church to share in the task at every level, as individual neighbours, as parishes and regions. The closing of the old institutions is a test of whether a community exists at all. Our argument ranged over whether ordinary people could play a part. Some thought it all needed to be done by the experts. But while we recognized the need for professional care and for proper asylum for really disturbed people, we also knew that there were many mentally sick people who were not violent or disturbed but just needed befriending, accepting and being allowed to join in. We also recognized how much support their relatives needed. Although many fears were expressed we really knew, because of Christ, we have no choice. Jesus spent a lot of love and energy on the mentally sick and bound up their wounds, and sometimes by miracle freed them from suffering.

As Terry said, explaining why he went back into such danger to try to obtain the release of the hostages, when all other support fails, in the love of Christ you just have to go on. The success of care in the community depends a great deal on government and on professionals, but it also depends on ordinary people like you and me to ensure that there is a community to care.

CAMERA CONFESSION

8 July 1992

Although sometimes it's a great comfort to think of God watching over me, there's also a rather solemn side to this faith. God sees us as we are, sees what we do, and knows our motives. But what makes it even more threatening is Jesus' teaching that everything we do in secret will be exposed to the light and made known.

I was reminded of this from a rather unexpected source – the recently implemented Road Traffic Act. Under its provisions, cameras will photograph any car travelling at excessive speed. A police spokesman admitted that if, in one journey, a car was photographed four times in different places, the driver could lose his or her licence. So without any direct and specific warning, that could mean the end of driving, the end of a job, the end of a way of life. If this happens, I'm sure drivers will shout 'Foul! ...We weren't given the chance to repent on the M1, the M6 and the M5 before we were condemned for carelessness.' There's no doubt, however, that where the cameras are used in this way, speeds have been reduced and lives saved – and we have all been warned about speeding so many times. But I know from my own experience that a severe dressing-down from a policeman slowed me up. If, after the first offence, a driver is punished, he or she might well be deterred from further offences. The magic eye means that drivers lose these chances for amendment of life. I suspect that many of us argue, 'Well, as long as I drive safely, it's OK to go above the speed limit, even if it's not strictly legal.' But we should never count ourselves as exempt from the law – that's the thin end of a very dangerous wedge. Also, we might think we're driving safely, but how can we know what's going to happen next at such speed?

When it comes down to it, it's the fear of detection which concentrates the mind – as we see when a police car comes into the traffic stream and all the cars try to brake without being noticed. Now with the cameras we shan't know we're being watched, and speeding 'sins' will be laid bare before the eyes of the law.

In moral terms, the undetected wrong is just as bad as the one which becomes a publicly exposed and punished offence. Yet our conscience is easier on us if we're not found out and the offence becomes just that bit easier to commit next time – like the businessperson whose fraud escapes detection, or the thief who gets away with a string of burglaries without being caught. But secret, undisclosed sins are just as bad in God's eyes, and in the end they will all be brought to the light. I just thank God he's a God of mercy.

UNISEX HUMANS?

28 October 1992

When I was thirteen I remember standing in front of a mirror putting make-up on, imitating the way my mother used to put on her lipstick. I was preparing to play Emilia in *Othello*. Like Shakespeare, our producer only had males for his cast. Emilia is a fine part – but although I generated passion, I had no idea, from a woman's point of view, what Emilia was thinking and feeling: her despising of her husband, her grief for her murdered mistress Desdemona, and her rage at Othello. Let's face it, if you had to cast *Othello* you'd rather Judi Dench played Emilia than Jim Thompson – though I'm sure I'd be a wow.

Yesterday a report was published by the Equal Opportunities Commission called 'An Equal Start'. It tries to combat sex-stereotyping among the under-eights. It warns teachers against using expressions like 'Big boys don't cry' because we big boys know we do, and it makes clear that the Wendy House must be open for boys as well as girls – even if the boys do hog the play-ground. I see the point of these warnings, because they free children to develop their own individuality. But I think that sometimes the argument can be taken too far and almost deny any complementarity of male and female, and suggest that, like hairdressers, humanity is unisex.

The other day I went to bless a new fire engine and met the fire crews. There was one woman in the group. Apparently it has not been easy to recruit women because some men fear that if the physical qualifications are reduced to include women it might lower the standards. Also, some women who might be interested don't apply because they themselves can't break the stereotype. But when fire crews are called to a major fire or a motorway accident, strength and height will be needed for part of the task and not necessary for others. If a person is being pulled from burning wreckage in severe shock, different gifts are needed. No doubt I shall get letters saying I'm stereotyping again, putting the women into the 'tender loving care' trap, and am just a victim of fifty-six years of 'Big boys don't cry'. But I don't think I am. I'm just trying to affirm complementarity in the sexes, not trying to argue against men doing the cooking and nursing, nor trying to stop women becoming builders, but rather asking that we don't have to denigrate half of God's treasury of human gifts.

Whatever happens in the Church of England's debate on the ordination of women next month, I hope that no woman will be forced into a mould men have created as leaders of the Church through 2,000 years. Whether as priests or deacons, we need women to be truly themselves.

Emilia and Desdemona were both victims, but the women who now play them are not, and play their full part on the world's stage – without, like Portia, having to pretend to be a man.

———————◆———————

FALSE WITNESS

16 February 1993

The Bishop's Palace at Wells has its own dungeon. The slits in the battlements look out across the moat. The dungeon is getting its twentieth-century spring clean, and beneath the pigeon grime we can now read the two tablets of stone on the walls, and there inscribed are the ten commandments. So the prisoners obviously sat and reflected upon the folly of their ways, in the light of the appropriate law of Moses.

Some people say that we don't hear enough of the ten commandments nowadays – 'We need the good, simple faith, Bishop.' I tend to agree, but I like to insist that we have the whole ten, because there's a tendency to choose the ones we ourselves are not tempted to break. The shaft of light in the dungeon shone on one which is most often ignored: 'Thou shalt not bear false witness.' The setting for this commandment was the judgement seat where the elders of the village, town or city would hear cases brought before them. So it's rather like 'You shall speak the truth, the whole truth and nothing but the truth.' To bear false witness was not only to pervert the course of justice, but also to damage a person's reputation on the basis of false evidence. But the commandment has a far wider application than just legal matters. It covers the nasty bits of gossip in the village shop, through to the lies and misrepresentations which happen in the press, where character assassination seems to be almost commonplace. Without wishing to curtail the freedom of the press on which a free society so much depends, some form of account- ability for bearing false witness, which does not depend on long and costly libel proceedings, would be a good corrective to the misuse of that precious freedom.

The line between proper and improper investigation can be a narrow one. When people are found guilty before the case has been fairly heard and where evidence is illegally obtained, or if not illegally then immorally by deception or indecent intrusion into people's privacy, I believe there should be some redress. We are all caught up in this because we read the papers and the apologies are tucked away in a corner, so a wider injustice takes place. False witness also breeds corruption because of the fear and suspicion that enter into human relationships via the phone tap or the telephoto lens. There are, of course, people who have the freedom and the money to fight back, but there are so many who could never afford to take action to defend themselves. But whatever the legal provision, the commandment remains clear to any person of faith. It is an offence against God to bear false witness, and the text should not only be on the walls of our dungeon, but in editors' offices and cutting rooms.

AWE-FILLED SCIENCE
AND RELIGION

17 February 1993

As we are hearing this week in the *Today* programme, the American Association for the Advancement of Science is meeting in Boston to discuss the origins of life. I have been excited by reading the reports. They have confirmed my belief that while science can neither prove nor disprove the existence of God, the true scientific spirit and the true religious spirit should have a great deal in common. It was Einstein who said, 'The most beautiful and profound emotion we can experience is the sensation of the mystical. He who can no longer wonder and stand wrapped in awe is as good as dead.'

Because of the developments of the Big Bang theory and the renewal of the belief in the significance of humankind, people who pray can begin to feel they are engaged in a partly similar search to the person looking down a microscope. One of the speakers in Boston claimed that in a human being there's 'a higher level of organization and richness than in a thousand lifeless galaxies'.

I'm not talking about falsifying science or the Bible to try to fit them together, but opening up the real possibility of God to the contemporary mind in a way which doesn't do violence to our reason, but opens a gate beyond it. When St John wrote, 'In the beginning was the Word and the Word was God; through him all things were made', he was not making a scientific statement but proclaiming a religious and mystical vision of Creation. Yet somehow this vision is enriched by the lecturer's claim that 'the greatest complexity in the universe is not the atomic structure nor the galactic scale, but the human brain'.

For so long, religious truths have been disregarded as though there was a fundamental contradiction between science and religion. This split in our personality has damaged the sense of wonder which is so essential to the human mind, the earth we inhabit and our influence on the universe. If religion and science were humble towards each other, we might open up new horizons of the human spirit.

Science often seems beyond the reach of those of us who have no training, but we can all explore our inner self – our soul. We can all contemplate the starry heavens above and watch the lily unfold. We can all make time and space to be open to God.

May I quote Einstein again and dare to paraphrase something he said? To know that what we cannot perceive really exists, manifesting itself as the highest wisdom and the most radiant beauty, which our dull faculties can only comprehend in the most primitive forms: this is knowledge, this feeling is the centre of true religion.

JAMES BULGER'S CALL

18 February 1993

Every day this week we've heard more about the murder of James Bulger. Although our minds are numb with terrible stories, this has really penetrated our defences. From the moment James left his mother's side to yesterday's arrests and releases and the rage of the crowds, there has been the sickening feeling that not only has a terrible crime been committed on a small boy, but in all likelihood, it was committed by children who only just over ten years ago were two-year-olds themselves.

Crimes committed by children in their early teens are not isolated events and they induce panic feelings that all the safety boundaries of behaviour have been shattered. We look immediately for who is to blame, and when we discover it's a child, we feel we need to look beyond the individual's wickedness. We want to ask, how did this young person travel from toddler to criminal in those childhood years? All parents know that children are capable of nastiness, but when they lose all moral sense we blame the parents or lack of parents, because we assume that it's in the home that the child has been brutalized by violence, hatred or just terrifying inadequacy. We all know that even in the best circumstances being a parent is hard and that too many people are totally unprepared for its demands. But our experience tells us that it is at home that the problem begins. Yet it's not just the lack of home love or the mistakes or absence of parents: the phenomenon of children's crime poses a great critique of our society – the values we operate, and our social priorities. We pound children with violence on television – our heads jangle with shattering glass, the crashing of cars, the sickening thud of boot against head. Today the unemployment figures will be announced to be over three million, with all the pressure that brings to a home. We propagate such shallow materialistic values, and above all we fail to share with our children the love of God.

Too many children grow up on a diet of loveless insecurity and their fragile moral antennae are vandalized beyond repair. They know of nowhere that they are valued, and therefore do not know how to respect others, and they are war veterans by the time they're ten.

It's so important that little James did not die in vain. If we can't get parents to be responsible for providing the children with a secure identity or some assurance that there is a place of safety and affection, many more of us have to be willing to work directly with children on a voluntary and professional basis.

I had lunch yesterday with a young community worker who has just started working with kids in East London. I asked him why. He said two things which somehow seem relevant and hopeful. 'To make the world a better place,' he said, and 'to provide a male role model for boys who have no fathers or fathers they despise, and to try to help them see there is another way.' I praise God for him and hope that James Bulger will call an army of such people.

———————◆———————

THE URBAN FARM

11 May 1993

This week in the *Observer* there was a brilliant photo. It showed a small boy standing on a rustic fence watching three cows in a field, feeding from a hay rack. But the backdrop, like a mirage, was Canary Wharf. The picture was taken in the Mudchute – an urban farm in the heart of Docklands. Like other urban farms, the Mudchute has financial problems. Just as many creative initiatives in our society, the accounts only show the cash and have no way of recording the value in people's lives. To relate in a wholesome way to nature is a way of drawing close to God and can teach a greater reverence for his creation.

I remember so well seeing those films of the post-war years – *Lassie Come Home*, *My Friend Flicka*. They had a great impact on us, even if Elizabeth Taylor's first romance with Pie in *National Velvet* was a little over the top. Then later there was *Kes*, where a boy befriends a kestrel, and you can see how his spirit soars away from the hard reality of the dark satanic mills. In all these stories, the child found in an animal a deep bonding, a friend to trust, to hug, to share secrets with – about parents and teachers and fears and imaginings.

Of course, it's not just children. I remember visiting a hospital where each ward had been given a pet. An old, bedridden lady was being comforted by stroking a purring cat lying on her bed. So often pets are not allowed in the places where they are most needed emotionally. But we all know people – perhaps ourselves

– who have found a pet to be a child substitute, a bereavement counsellor, a companion in loneliness and someone to talk to. Although we can be potty about our pets, I believe that in God's eyes our relationships with animals, involving as they do eternal values such as friendship, love and trust, have a spiritual content.

Isaiah's vision of the Kingdom of God speaks of a harmony in creation, and children are mentioned twice – the calf and the young lion will feed together with a little child to tend them, and the infant will play over the cobra's nest. They will not hurt or destroy in all God's holy mountain.

Country people live in close touch with nature and with animals, and the children learn about birth and death, fun and grief, as just a natural part of growing up. Yet in the inner cities and the urban sprawl, there's much brutalizing of children who live in heartless places with heavy street rules where cruel spirits are born. So the urban farms are a small but precious step in providing children in urban areas with opportunities to grow up with animals, and to experience much-needed affection.

JONATHAN

12 May 1993

Recently I went to visit a baby – Jonathan – in hospital. He had been baptized on the day he was born, because the doctors thought he was going to die. When I saw him, he had had several major operations and his little body looked like a space experiment, with tubes and pipes emerging from every nook and cranny. The nurse told me there was only one bodily function that he was doing for himself – and he was doing that splendidly! I sat by him for half an hour and felt very aware of God; being next to this fragile but tough little human being, you couldn't help but pray. As I meditated on this, I looked at all the machines and computers keeping his systems going. The nurse explained some of them to me – the monitoring, the engineering and the feeding. It struck me how wonderful a thing a normal baby is. All the systems, which require all that machinery and technology when they go wrong, normally go right. They are all neatly packed in a tiny frame and wrapped in flesh – a miraculous breathing, digesting, cleansing, communicating, feeling, intelligent system. It's awe-inspiring. No wonder the psalmist gasped, 'I am fearfully and wonderfully made' – 'you, O Lord, knit me together in my mother's womb'. Seeing what was needed to restore Jonathan to health made me realize how much we take for granted in normality. We walk and leap, we calculate and balance, we see and hear when all is well. Yet so often we treat all that amazing potential, that prodigious technological gift as if we had created it ourselves.

As Jonathan's parents watched his chest heaving, as he recovered from the invasions of his small body, and they looked at the scars of such comprehensive surgery, they must have thought: 'What sort of life will he have if he survives?' Well, it will unfold and depend on the long-term effects of the trauma he's been through. But there are no machines, no technology that can make him a person: they can only provide the wherewithal, in which and through which his personality will grow. They can't create a sense of humour, courage to face grief, they can't make him loving; machines can't make him hopeful, they can't make him good. All those virtues, and indeed his vices, will be the result of the journey of his soul with the God who made him and his parents who love him.

The other day we celebrated Jonathan's earlier baptism in church. There he was, looking strong and healthy and one hundred per cent DIY.

GOD AND PREDATORY VIOLENCE

13 October 1993

One delight of where we live in Wells is the sighting of a flash of brilliant blue flying past our kitchen window as the kingfisher comes to its perch on the laburnum tree. We see it dive into the water – but when it catches a fish it beats it to death. I might like kingfishers, but the fish don't.

I watched a programme on television about three cheetahs who were brothers who prowled around the Serengeti like *The Professionals*. In introducing the programme, the announcer warned nervous viewers that the film contained 'scenes of predatory violence'. I thought: what else should we expect to see if we follow three cheetahs round the Serengeti? Cheetahs, like kingfishers and much of the natural world, survive or die by predatory violence.

Yet so many people seem to deny and cover up the cruelty. They want to treat nature as if the prophecy of Isaiah was already fulfilled or ought to be – that the wolf shall lie down with the lamb, and the infant play over the viper's nest. But the sight of a newborn gazelle calf, nuzzling up to one of the cheetahs which was toying with it prior to the kill, made it shockingly clear just how predatory and vicious the system can be.

It raises for me questions about God and about ourselves. Those of us who believe in a loving God have to come to terms with the fact that God made the Creation dependent upon predatory violence for the balance that makes life possible on earth. But we all have to think about where the human species fits in. We are the most effective and violent predators of all. We leave fish to flap and heave their way to death on deck; we take our chickens from the freezer without a thought as to how they lived or died; we kill insects and what we call pests; we shoot, hunt and trap all manner of animals, as human beings have always done. We also engage in predatory violence against each other, with the endless wars, the fascination with cops and robbers, last night's behaviour of football fans in Amsterdam, and the predatory search for sexual satisfaction. I was always more aware of predatory violence in the city than in the countryside.

We don't seem to know how to deal with this insistent genetic inheritance. We seem to be suspended between the animal kingdom as chief predator, and being possessors of our human conscience and self-awareness. To understand our role in God's creation we need to abandon a prissy, sentimental view of nature and look again at what is the proper human relationship to it. Both the kingfisher and the fisherman kill fish, but before we judge either we might remember that God appears to have made it so.

FOOTBALL HOOLIGANS

14 October 1993

As we have heard, there was no trouble in Amsterdam overnight, but we have vivid newspaper reports on the night before. The violence continued into the early hours with fans gathering in groups of up to a hundred and making charges up the narrow streets, causing damage and punching passers-by. Two policemen injured and five hundred arrests. Why do they do it? We comprehend less and want to punish more. We call it 'thuggery', 'mindless violence' – and so it is. It stains a victory or, in this case, compounds the defeat. It reminded me of young offenders who, on television, gave their own reasons for their crimes. One of the motives they described was the need to gain respect. They stole cars and drove them at great speed, rammed shops, risked their lives to gain the respect of their mates. Presumably some of the same dynamic was at work in the visit to the red light district of Amsterdam and the ensuing clash with the police. Somehow they belong to the group and want its respect. Many of us remember the passionate desire for the respect of our friends – the cigarette behind the bike-shed, the under-age visit to the pub, the dangerous dares. I remember being ashamed because I was afraid of tackling on the rugger field, and I grew a foot in height when I finally learnt I could do it. So many ways to gain our incentives.

But if the role models, the values, the heroes are distorted, then respect for them itself becomes perverting. And where do these young males learn what to respect? Certainly from the adult males in their lives. We've heard a lot about absent fathers, but I've seen so much damage done by violent, aggressive, immoral fathers, stepfathers or just the men in their lives. So much of the way we learn respect comes early and is then stoked by peer group expectations. The macho male model is a familiar old lie.

But it's also learnt from the culture. It's not a culture into which most of us Radio 4 people gain any access. It's a culture where there's not much else which earns respect, where there's little opportunity to discover personal worth, where self-respect has not been taught or learnt. It's a culture nurtured by violent videos, by booze, by the gutter press. But it has its own distorted morality, having little stake in more normal acceptable behaviour. We fool ourselves if we think our disgust or even their punishments are going to stop it. We need good parenting and an army of men and women who will go out of their way to get alongside, share and understand the culture, become trusted in it and provide alternative good models. To concentrate on punishment alone can encourage their respect for the lawlessness we are trying to prevent.

THREE KINGS

21 December 1993

I was just setting off to preach at a carol service on the Somerset Levels, when the phone rang. Did I believe in the three wise men, because the Bishop of Durham probably didn't? The press had received a long statement, and wanted to know my views. I thought – I'm not going to indulge in this absurd game of reducing the profound faith of two thousand years to a sound-bite. So I drove off into the rain to the village church of Chedzoy, where the candlelight flickered up to the nave roof, and touched the faces of the holy family, the shepherds, and the wise men worshipping, like us, at the cradle rude and bare. As the greatest story ever told began to unfold in carols and readings, those three mysterious figures, students of the night sky, bringing their precious gifts with their deeper meaning, seemed so valuable. They were communicating the truth the Church is always trying to communicate: that Christ is God from God and Light from Light. Through the gold we learn he is a King. Through the frankincense we know we are drawing near to God, and through the myrrh we are warned that suffering and death are intrinsic to the life of this man born to be King.

Did I believe whether it was historically true, as I do most of the Gospel story? At any rate, we can never know. We do know that Mary was present at Jesus' death and was a witness to the resurrection. She would have reflected on all that had happened and talked it over with the apostles and maybe with the people who made the first record of the events. So, looking back to his birth, I would expect the people of their day to tell it, partly through known facts and partly by expressing, in their way, the meaning of the thing. No amount of argument can tell us for certain whether the three wise men are fact or meaning or both.

Part of the trouble is our use of the word 'myth'. We usually mean something which turns out to be untrue, a sort of self-deception, but myths can carry great truths as well as falsehoods – for better, for worse. The myth of Aryan supremacy gave Hitler justification for Nazi tyranny, and the myths of Olympia still conjure up for us the highest excellence in sport. It looks as though the myth of Chairman Mao is about to be severely dented, but he did take part in the Long March. It seems as though myths are highly effective for good or ill; indeed, perhaps the well-being of a society depends upon the myths which motivate its people. Whether the three wise men are one of Mary's secrets or St Matthew's theological genius, or a bit of both, their truth is wonderfully beneficial for us today in a society which, above all, needs a sense of worship, reverence and wonder.

BRAVING BARRICADES

22 December 1993

Have you ever noticed how often dogs attack other dogs which are in cars or behind a fence? They often bark and snarl and even rush up and down . . . whereas if they met on their afternoon walk, they would probably just sniff politely. Our dog has carried it to an art form. He climbs up onto our thirty-foot-high battlements and, balancing on the parapets, he abuses passers-by. From the safety of his fortress, our friendly little springer becomes a macho mastiff.

In many ways we are just the same. I used to know a lady who hated black people. Then one day a West Indian couple moved in next door. She got to know them and they became firm friends. When I pointed this out, she said, 'Ah yes, but it's those Asians and Pakistanis I can't stand.' We can be so brave and aggressive, behind walls, in ways we never would be, face to face. The more anonymous the person is the more aggressive we seem willing to be – shouting down telephones at officials, tearing faceless bureaucrats apart in distant prose. But the difficulty is that they all have faces, and bleed the same as we do. The fortress mentality hardens hearts made hard by the battlements which divide them.

On a recent visit to Belfast I caught a glimpse of what it must be like to recognize that the barricades have become part of the furniture. Some are made of barbed wire or corrugated iron; some, like the peace line that divides Catholics and Protestants, some have been scarred into people's minds by tragedy, others expressed in graffiti; but for everyone – barricades. After a visit to the troops, I was expressing some sympathy for the conditions in which they lived and the way of life which was forced upon them. In a quiet voice my Belfast friend said: 'You don't know how hard it is for me to hear this.' It was a world away from the usual thoughts she had about the troops, and as a band marched past, I wondered how their minds were ever going to be changed about the people who lived just across the road. Yet in spite of the apparent impossibility, I caught a real feeling of hope from the many people who were crossing the barricades and attempting to hear the people whom they found it hard to hear. From behind the barricades they seem so alien and threatening, but they all bleed the same, they all have names.

I came away with so many questions, but the main one was: how does faith in Jesus Christ affect it all? St Paul depicts him as breaking down the walls of division, removing the barricades, working towards a single undivided humanity. So we may hope he is in every attempt to find peace, in every prayer, in every person who has the courage to take down the walls of their personal and corporate fortress, and see people face to face.

DISCONCERTING MANHOOD

23 December 1993

I found it irritating, while doing the washing-up, to listen to the responses to the latest survey on household duties. I don't know which niggled me more – the fact that I still manage to do so little, or the representative man who was interviewed and said he never did household duties . . . that's why he had a wife. I was interested to read that women claim to be happier than men, especially if they work in addition to doing the bulk of the household chores. This seems to suggest that, even if women are a long way short of their goal, they at least have an idea where they're going, whereas men seem so unsure. Perhaps that's why men defend their territory so fiercely in the boardroom, the police force and the Church. At least as breadwinner, or manufacturer or businessman we seemed relatively secure, but now women work in the fire service, are executives and priests. I share the dilemma, recognizing what a funny mixture I am. For instance, when I watched the All Blacks doing the Maori haka, and even more amazing, when I saw England beat them, I was thrilled, and I thought, 'That's what it's like to be a man.' But then I was also thrilled to hear about a husband who was helping in the delivery of his wife's baby. They had to use surgery, so that when the baby was born, the mother was not able to nurse the child. The man was told to take off his shirt and hold the baby against his skin. It was a great moment in his life; it did not diminish his manhood, rather it expressed his own deep feelings. Old certainties are shaking and it can leave men demoralized and confused. I guess that's one reason why some men still think it's manly to harass gays, because in a way they represent such a confusing image of masculinity.

Oversimplified male identikits do not help. We have to discover what it means to be a man in our own day. It always fascinates me how difficult many men in our society find Jesus, whereas in many other cultures he is seen to be profoundly manly. He appears to me to possess plenty of characteristics which men can identify with – dignity, courage, reverence for God; his compassion, his care for truth and justice. Christians are now celebrating his manhood as well as his humanity. But perhaps it's hard for some to accept his unwillingness to fight back, his celibacy, his love and his acceptance of the crown of thorns. As Pilate said, 'Behold the man.' Finding what manhood is today is demanding, even disconcerting; but also liberating if we are genuinely open to the future and accept our vulnerability. As I finished the script my working wife finished the ironing.

DIS-ARMING EVIL

8 March 1994

A street in Gloucester has suddenly had its normality blown apart. We can only feel sympathy for the victims, their friends and relatives, and hope there's some relief for those involved, in being able to bring their loved ones to rest in a sacred place. But Cromwell Street is not alone in this, because the horror being quarried out of the house affects us all. It goes with all the other plunges into the nightmare side of human experience – the degrading, the violent and pornographic commonplace of our daily news.

In ancient days the people had great myths by which evil could be identified and warded off. For them the roots of evil were supernatural – even if they were nurtured in the human mind. But for most of us the ancient pictures carry a credibility gap, and we tend to find the cause simply in those who perpetuate the evil. Whoever murdered the seven women discovered so far had a mind so depraved as to repeat again and again such evil deeds. It seems inconceivable that such an evil imagination could present a normal face to the world. We know that the human imagination can be profoundly corrupted, and we've seen how horrific it is when evil fantasies are translated into fact. No doubt many will see there's no other agent in this than an evil personality. But I'm not sure. I know from the wrong things I've done, it's remarkable how well the inner tempter is tuned to deceive me and lure me to sin. It was André Gide who warned us against letting go of the devil just because of his antique vesture! He was convinced that there was a 'more than human' source of evil. But whether it is just the way we are, or there is a personal malevolent force such as satan, evil is real and devastating in human lives – whether just the petty sins of a normal life in a normal street, or the horrendous crimes from the nightmare side.

Christianity is very clear in its treatment of evil. Jesus himself is portrayed in constant battle with the evil one – sometimes addressing it directly, sometimes just wrestling with the power of it in human lives, but the Gospel – the good news – is that the light shines on in the darkness and the darkness will never overcome it. The promise is that Christ can rout the evil in the human soul and disarm the cosmic powers. So, though we have to face the severity of evil, we can live in faith that the power of love and goodness is ultimately greater.

UNMENTIONABLES

15 March 1994

We learnt yesterday that only one in six sufferers from incontinence consults an expert. The reason – fear of embarrassment. An excellent new campaign asks, 'Why suffer in silence?' It aims to free people from the fear of telling and get them access to proper treatment.

When I think back to childhood, a whole range of things were never mentioned. My aunt's hot flushes, sanitary towels, sperms, masturbation – even bottoms could be considered difficult in company. I remember that terrible time when I tried to ask the doctor about my 'uhum' without mentioning it by name. When I look back I think how crazy we were to be so shy about our private functions and the embarrassment incurred in mentioning the unmentionable. Yet I guess it was all to protect us – or was it to protect our parents? It now seems so much more sensible to be free and open about it all, because secrecy caused considerable isolation and fear. For thousands of years various taboos operated, often reinforced by religious sanctions. In the Book of Leviticus there are detailed instructions on how to cope with the supposed uncleanness of menstruation, and people with damaged organs were not allowed to worship with the people of God. Even when I was first a priest in East London there were still women who would not go out in public until they'd been churched after childbirth.

Food was another taboo-affected area, but Jesus questioned the whole principle: 'Nothing that goes into a person from outside can defile him. It's what comes out of a person that defiles him . . . from inside . . . from the human heart.' St Mark comments, knowing full well how scandalous his words would be: 'By saying this Jesus declared all foods clean.' But Jesus went further, allowing himself to be seen eating with, touched by, people whom he knew were judged unclean. In his care for others he would not protect himself or his reputation. But then I thought, with all our contemporary freedom from taboos, had we gone too far? Is there privacy we should preserve? Are there actions we should be afraid of, experiments we should not make, boundaries we should not cross? A farmer told me that the Minister would not now have to defend British beef, if we had not broken nature's rules for herbivorous cows. And when you see smokers herded into the smoking compartment on a train or cast out for anti-social behaviour, I wonder if this is a new secular taboo. Perhaps we could develop taboos against racist bigotry, or mistreatment of children. There are God-given limits which should not be exceeded, not in any way to persecute people or make than outcasts, but rather to protect people and society. There are times when we need to be warned of the consequences of ignoring our maker's instructions.

WELLS SPRINGS

22 March 1994

Yesterday I was sitting in lovely sunshine watching the water bubbling up from the Wells springs in the Bishop's garden. At the moment the supply is so great it cascades down the waterfall into the moat. In 1450 Bishop Beckington decided to provide running water for the city and laid pipes from his pump house to take the water for cleansing down the gutters of the High Street. As I enjoyed the spring day – the daffodils, primroses and weeping willows and the tufted duck happily diving in the flood – my mind raced back eleven years to Namibia. There, after five years' drought, a group of us travelled to the war-torn North in severe heat. The rivers and water holes were dried up and the cattle like skeletons. We arrived at our destination, dehydrated and exhausted, and our host shocked us all by offering us a shower. We relished the water running over our bodies and never for a moment thought of it running away down the drain. I asked our beleaguered host how they managed for water, and he said, 'We knew you liked showers so we saved the water for three months.' Ever since then I've had a totally different view of water: not only because of the generous sacrifice of our hosts, but because of the shame of taking it for granted day by day.

Today is United Nations World Day of Water. In that world two billion people lack safe water to drink; 25,000 children die daily from water-related diseases, and often women and children walk miles in blazing heat to fetch their basic water supply. It's a matter of life or death. It's fundamental to our very being, as I know to my cost after being in a dehydration coma later in that Namibian trip.

As we look out on the developing world and see the repeated pictures of famine and poverty caused by war and drought, we can feel so impotent. But we needn't. It's wonderful to see people selling the vegetables they have grown on their land, rather than begging for food. It's encouraging to see the steps being taken against bilharzia – responsible for so much illness and death. It's magic to see a village transformed by a new well. All these things can be done – so we don't need to feel helpless.

The Bible was mostly written in a very hot and dry climate, so it's not surprising that water is often used to describe the blessing of God. In foretelling the coming of the Kingdom of God, Isaiah says this: 'On that day you will all draw water from the wells of deliverance . . . the mirage will become a pool, the thirsty land bubbling springs.' As I sat watching the spring bubbling in our garden, I thought that what Bishop Beckington did for the city of Wells in 1450, we could do for the world by 2000.

TRAINERS OR GOLDEN LILIES

7 September 1994

A friend of mine took her six-year-old daughter to buy school shoes. Every pair was rejected. 'They hurt.' 'My friends don't have to wear shoes like that.' 'I'm sure the Mickey Mouse trainers would be all right.' Mum felt vulnerable, because she could foresee hideous tantrums; she knew her powerlessness, but she was determined – so she said, 'You'll have to wear your Wellingtons to school and the trainers only indoors.' But the victory was with the six-year-old. She had realized her power. The loving, caring mum had tried to be strict, but had few sanctions.

This story brought to mind a passage from *Wild Swans* – a book about three generations of Chinese women in which a two-year-old girl was made to have her feet bound so that she would be able to wear three-inch golden lilies – three-inch-long shoes – when she was a grown woman. Her mother wound a piece of white cloth, about twenty inches long, around her feet, bending all the toes except the big toe, inward and under the sole. Then she placed a large stone on top, to crush the arch. The process lasted several years. Even after the bones had been broken, the feet had to be bound day and night. The girl would weep with excruciating pain but she was always told it was for her own future happiness. Only with minute feet would she get a husband.

Yesterday I saw a pair of three-inch golden lilies, and they are an ornate but terrifying witness to what the weight of tradition, male domination and absolute authority can do to a child's feet. Perhaps the TV film shown yesterday of Chinese girl babies lying dead in the street because they are surplus to the state rule of one child per mother, is a by-product of this horrific past.

Looking at the Mickey Mouse trainers of the six-year-old, able to out-gun her mother in a power struggle, and the three-inch bone crushers of absolute tradition, I wonder where the right sort of authority lay? We can see the cruelty of compression and crippling the Chinese girls to satisfy male desire, but we're less clear about how to treat the six-year-old in our own time and place. Parenting is difficult enough, but often made worse by culture and peer group pressure. The Christian faith teaches the importance of respect for adults, and also demands of adults proper respect for children – but freedom and responsibility grow as the child grows. There are boundaries which have to be asserted and the shoes have to fit, yet allow room for growth. Ultimate authority lies with mum – until, well, until it doesn't!

THE SINKING OF THE *ESTONIA*

28 September 1994

As I was coming into Bristol to do 'Thought for the Day', I heard the news of the *Estonia*'s sinking in heavy seas at about one o'clock this morning. There was a glimpse of terror as the last message said, 'We are listing twenty degrees, thirty degrees' – and then silence. Then we were left to imagine the huge weight of containers and lorries lurching the ship to disaster. It all happened so quickly – the nightmare of the thrashing seas, with children and men and women screaming with fear – and then for them, silence. Thankfully, some have been rescued and more may yet be picked up by the boats and helicopters as it gets light.

We are listening as fairly dispassionate observers hearing of yet another tragedy round the world, but the people in Sweden and the rest of Scandinavia will be listening to hear if one of their loved ones was on board – with a different level of commitment and dread.

Strangely, I was going to speak about the harvest and remind us all of the continuous miracle of the abundant generosity of God in the Creation, and suddenly we're faced with the tragic down-side of the natural world in which we live. The water which brings life to the harvest, which makes the valleys stand thick with corn, is the water which heaves in the stormy seas and suffocates the sinking ship. As with all the elemental things in nature, there is this ambiguity. The fire that warms us and gives us power is the fire that burns and kills. The story of our human life is in part the struggle with frightening ambiguities. For some, this takes away the rationality of God – would God allow such grief and tragedy to be written into the whole system? Isn't it more like a chaotic accident? But others – and I'm one of them – believe that it is part of the way God makes freedom possible; that without the struggle, without the dark side, we would be a sort of plastic creation, not knowing courage, hope, love, trust – a brave new world anaesthetized against pain.

But these words will not be a comfort to all who have lost loved ones in the *Estonia*. We just pray that in their grief they'll find that slow, healing comfort which comes from faith that those they've lost are not lost to the love of God in eternity. It's not like a sedative – more a matter of intimate comfort from the God who created it all from the beginning.

Note. This was written on my knee, as my driver drove over the Mendips to the studio in Bristol . . . the shortest notice I have ever been given.

MOTHER TERESA

9 November 1994

First we were told that Albert Schweitzer fell short of his legendary goodness in his medical work and his attitudes to black Africa, and now Mother Teresa has been subject to harsh criticism in Christopher Hitchens' TV programme last night called *Hell's Angel*. In an article he wrote: 'Only an absence of scrutiny has allowed her to pass unchallenged as a force for pure goodness.' He claims it's high time we all come to our senses. So we were shown her association with dictators and corrupt political regimes, her worldwide travels, her strong opposition to abortion and contraception. She was described as a demagogue, an obscurantist and a servant of earthly powers.

Whether these criticisms are justified we don't know. We don't know what her motives are, and she was not asked. We know, however, that she has struggled with a situation that would defeat most of us. We know too that she has been an encouragement and inspiration to millions of people around the world. Now aged eighty-four, with most of her struggles behind her, with arteries hardened and less flexible in body and spirit, she has got the full cynical treatment. It's difficult to avoid a feeling of disappointment. This passionate desire to strip away the reputation of our icons, because they got some things wrong, leaves the sense that something sacred has again been defaced and another symbol of hope shattered.

Mr Hitchens is concerned with Mother Teresa's reputation as a force for pure goodness. I began to think what pure goodness might be. Have you ever met it? Some of the greatest and holiest people I have known show how complicated goodness can be. It can emerge from lifelong battles with weakness, from forgiveness of sins – including murder. Much goodness grows in the ambiguity of personality. Monks and nuns I have known often experience intense battles between the good they long for and their own personal weaknesses. One of the best people I ever knew said to me just before she died: 'The trouble is people think too well of me.' She knew too much about herself and her journey, yet she really was a source of hope and vision for many of us.

When I scrabble around looking for any goodness there may be in my life, I'm horrified how it has been cobbled together out of slugs and snails and puppy-dogs' tails. I suggest that pure goodness in us is a fantasy – an impossible goal until we come into the presence of God. Here we live by his grace in our mess.

LOTTERY HALLELUJAH

16 November 1994

Much of the propaganda for the National Lottery hype has a hint of God in it. 'The chosen one' is seen looking out of the window at the night sky, when a divine starry outstretched arm reaches out to bless him with his million. And the 'Hallelujah Chorus' is used as the background music to the prize-giving. Before we know where we are, we shall be like Spain and, as we heard earlier, celebrate Christmas with the grand lottery of the Nativity. These intimations of divinity are not surprising because many people see the Lottery as a source of hope and the possible fulfilment of their dreams. 'If only I can find the mystical numbers, I shall enter paradise.'

A ticket gives a fourteen-million-to-one chance of winning. It also gives a donation of twenty-five pence so that, as the advert says, 'Someone else gets a better chance.' That's a lot less better chance than if we gave our pound to a decent charity which only spends ten pence on administration.

So here we are, with fourteen million tickets already sold and, because our nation is thought to be unwilling to raise the money by taxation, many good causes are going to rely on twenty-five per cent of a gambling pool – indeed, many of the concerns I am involved in will have to apply to the Lottery for funds. We are now a society that pays for equipment for disabled people, sports facilities for our children, our art, our heritage, from a Lottery: and thus we enter the third millennium on the basis of a giant game show with all the 'Oohs' and 'Ahs' of a vast studio audience – our brave new world.

To me, the idea that it brings hope and the fulfilment of dreams is even more deceptive. The Christian hope by comparison is not just for one winner in fourteen million, but is offered to all. Although religion has sometimes been 'Pie in the sky when you die', and accused therefore of being the opium of the people, the true hope of the Gospel is drawn from the love of God and the building of a just society based on spiritual values. Opium may relieve, for a moment, the pain of reality, but it is highly addictive and brings worse poverty in its wake. What I look for in the Queen's speech today is a basis for real down-to-earth hope – so that, for instance, people will not be sent home redundant without notice, will not be written off because they're forty-five or long-term unemployed. Now that would be a source of hope, fulfil many dreams, and justify a 'Hallelujah Chorus'.

SHORT/SHARK/SHOCK

30 November 1994

The other night I turned on the television and saw a middle-aged lady, standing in her bathing costume, enjoying the sun on the deck of a trawler in magnificent seas. Then she put on diving equipment and climbed into a cage, before plunging to the depths, to confront great white sharks with a short/shark/shock machine. The sharks veered off in spite of bleeding bait. Admittedly our heroine was a professional, but I was forced to think she must be a little bit mad. But I'm only a little less so. Two years ago, aged fifty-six, I took up riding, and my wife – who is much younger than me – joined my late middle-aged adventure. We recognize that riding horses can be dangerous – my limbs creak and would not prosper from coming down to earth. And we're normally quite cautious people; we watch our cholesterol, eat lots of greens, we don't drink or smoke or buy Lottery tickets, and here we are, week by week, clambering on board two potentially wild animals. It came to a head last week when both horses bolted. But I was so exhilarated by the experience; in a few years I'll probably be using my zimmer for a climbing frame.

So what is it that makes people go shark diving, climb mountains, run marathons, ride horses, long after it's sensible? We call it our Alternative Stress Therapy. It's wonderful how being afraid of falling off a large swift horse removes all other stress from the mind.

We spend most of our lives trying to be sensible and ultra-responsible and it's stressful, so it's marvellous therapy to release the adventurous, irresponsible self. Just because we have to behave like cautious, careful adults doesn't kill off the desire to take some risks and prove that the spirit of youth, if not the limbs, is still alive in us.

I see this as a parable of faith. If all we see in faith is nervous, careful inhibition, we can lose the divine spark of adventure which God has programmed into the thriving of our race. Jesus taught that, unless we become like a child, we shall not enter the Kingdom of Heaven – and even more dramatic words: 'Whoever wants to save his life will lose it, but whoever loses his life for my sake will save it.' I'm sure he didn't have riding horses in mind, but as the wind rushes past, I sense something like the excitement of faith.

PROUD TO BE BRITISH?

30 March 1995

As we've just heard, the Prince of Wales addressed the 'Britain in the World' conference yesterday in London. He challenged us to discover more proper pride in our country. Certainly his accusing of cynics and denigrators, who constantly undermine any confidence we possess, rang true to me, and the conference raised an even more basic question: what would make us proud to be British?

When I was a child, national pride seemed almost second nature – riding home on my bike cheering when Hitler was defeated, watching the Brabazon take off at Farnborough, studying the vast pink areas in the atlas. It all seemed more clearcut, more self-assured when Sylvia Peters read the news. But when you grow older everything seems more grey and complex. We don't know who to believe, have no easily identifiable enemies. We're not even sure whether to support Canada in the fishing dispute because of the Commonwealth and because the Canadians appear to be right, or Spain because of the European connection. It seems far more difficult to identify international rights and wrongs.

Perhaps we ought to have a national opinion poll to ask what does or would make us proud to be British. I've drawn up a list of my ten commitments. If I ruled the world, I would say to the United Kingdom:

1. Earn your living and give ten per cent away.
2. Share work more evenly and make more time for relationships, recreation and rest.
3. Be good, strong stewards of the planet earth.
4. Develop a culture of reverence for life and respect for each other.
5. Strive for integrity in public life and service.
6. Let justice be the foundation of order.
7. Pursue fidelity in human relationships.
8. Regard children as the central and primary responsibility of families and the community.
9. Stop valuing everything in money terms.
10. Be responsible, as individuals and as society, for the poor, the sick, the helpless.

All these ten commitments are clearly set out in the Bible and obviously have to be lived in the messy society we have created, so I would have to add a government health warning that all this depends upon discovering prayer, sacrifice, and the love of God. If these were our goals we could be called a faith-full country because we would be striving to make the United Kingdom more like the Kingdom of God.

Then I would be proud to be British.

THE ETHICS OF
PERSONAL TASTE

13 September 1995

Do you remember the wonderful Joyce Grenfell? Her teacher's soliloquy included the delicious line spoken to a small boy, 'George, don't do that.' We were never told what George was doing, but it was probably what this week's moral guidelines for the under-fives would call 'behaving inappropriately'.

I'm sure that in the days of Joyce Grenfell's teacher it was far easier to tell children what was right and wrong. Her school probably had a Latin motto and a foundation charter to guide her. But we live in a time of great moral uncertainty. We mostly do what we choose – if we can afford it – and only give an occasional nod in the direction of any moral absolutes. Everything is relative and, like the supermarket, largely a matter of personal taste.

According to the new nursery guidelines, the under-fives have to learn to take turns, to share fairly, to respect others, to treat property with care, and behave appropriately! I guess that most playgroup leaders and nursery teachers would think those were reasonably practical goals – a sort of lowest common denominator ethics giving no offence to parents, unions, atheists or people of other faiths. Perhaps that was all Sir Ron Dearing could ask in the moral maze.

This same moral uncertainty appears in adult form in the ICM poll for the *Guardian* on infidelity. For instance, one out of three people who've had affairs don't feel any guilt. For them, infidelity is no longer wrong – just a matter of opinion. It can, after all, improve one's sex life and act like an escape valve in boring relationships. Yet infidelity involves lying, deceit and betrayal; it is a threat to marriage and to steady relationships – and that's before it's revealed! If it's then discovered it causes grief, anger and perhaps years of pain and resentment. It can split parents and deprive children of fundamental security.

Both the guidelines for the under-fives and the poll on infidelity demonstrate the moral uncertainty of our day. I believe this is a result of trying to detach morality from God. It's as though it's in free fall. Almost every ethic is relative, where there's no outward point of reference, vision or judgement – apart from the law, public opinion, and our own desire.

Faithfulness, fidelity, is one of the most basic virtues associated with God's love for us, and is the rock on which our love of God is built. It can be taught as soon as the idea can be understood.

WHAT IS WORK?

20 September 1995

After church on Sunday I shook hands with a farmer. His hand was roughened by the hard graft of a farmer's life. Feeling my hand, with a twinkle in his eye, he said, 'I wouldn't offer you a job with hands like that!' 'Praise the Lord,' I said, 'I'm not looking for one.' His calloused hands represented long years of physical work on the land.

Last week I also visited a Benedictine priory. We talked about the work of monks and nuns. How should they divide their time between prayer and hospitality? St Benedict said that the Opus Dei – the work for God – should take precedence over all other work . . . to pray is to work.

In one of those exciting shifts of gear in a bishop's life, I had just visited the port of Avonmouth. There I toured the brilliantly renewed Portbury Dock. There is now a greater throughput of cars, feeding stuffs, toilet paper, coal, than in the days when the wharf was full of ships and thousands worked in the docks. The chairman took us into a new warehouse, and on the computer he operated a great grain silo which we saw moving to his instructions. At his touch, there was the power of a thousand dockers' hard-worn hands. The place seemed somewhat deserted but the import/export business in bulk went like clockwork.

Three types of work – the monk, the farmer and the chairman of the port. So, what is work? We tend to think of it as the job we're paid to do, but housewives aren't paid, monks are not paid, volunteers by definition are not paid. We tend to think of work as having boundaries, when we start and finish, but what of the woman or man who works all day and then goes home to clean, iron and cook? What about all the retired people who give their time to the community? I find it difficult to say when my work stops or starts. The edges are getting blurred, with people putting together bits of part-time work, people unable to find work, saving their self-respect by offering useful service.

Perhaps, like the monks and nuns, they are calling our bluff about work – looking at it in a different way. It's not new; if our lives are under the rule and love of God, our work is our service. We speak of the service industry, but isn't all work at best a service? Whether paid or not, whether eight-hour shift or all the waking hours, it's what we offer to God and to our community – whether unemployed, or housewife, or monk or farmer or chairman of a great port.

'ALL THAT STUFF ABOUT MIRACLES AND MYSTERIES'

13 December 1995

The Church of England has been celebrating the tenth anniversary of *Faith in the City*, its report on the urban priority areas. Roy Hattersley apparently read it again recently before preaching on the subject. He honours the report because it assumed that in a decent society it has a moral obligation to eliminate poverty. He concludes in a newspaper article, 'What a pity the Church of England persists with all that stuff about miracles and mysteries. Otherwise,' he says, 'it would be exactly the sort of political party that I would want to join.'

The difficulty is that 'all that stuff about miracles and mysteries' is, in a way, the heart of the matter. For instance, I hardly think the birth of Christ, robbed totally of mystery and miracle, would have captivated people of every age and nation. Sadly, there have been many children born in sheds, moved on as refugees, who have ended their lives in innocence on a cross. But the miracle of Jesus' birth, the music of heaven, the worship of the shepherds and the wise men, make it clear from the beginning that this is the Christ of God. It is the eternal love of God revealed in a helpless baby. It is the beauty and the mystery, the untarnished coming of God into his world, that bring hope. He embraced the suffering, identified with us, and gave his life for us. Then, at the place where all human defeat and despair are found, the greatest miracle and mystery of all opened the gate of Heaven.

All this 'religious stuff' is the motivation for loving the loveless, for touching the untouchable, for offering some hope even to the incurable, and this brings us back to *Faith in the City*. What made it so strong against racism but the vision of every human being as a precious child of God? What enabled the writers to see hope in places largely abandoned by society but the hope they saw in the resurrection? What inspired the demand for justice for the inner cities but the vision of the Kingdom of God, and what has empowered the action in these ten years but faith in God, who is Spirit. Now there seems to be such a chasm between the Christmas of the market place and the great miracle and mystery of the birth of Christ.

In facing the problems of our society now, this spiritual emptiness is what deprives us of the essential wonder and reverence for each other and for God, which could prevent and heal so many of our wounds, and shine light in the darkness.

FAMILY CHRISTMAS?

20 December 1995

If we were to visit the houses in our street or village this Christmas, we would find fifty-seven varieties of family. Some would be what a 'family' has come to mean – two parents and their children. But many would not. The 1993 figures for households in the UK reveal that twenty-seven per cent are single persons, thirty-five per cent are two persons, and if we add the percentage of single parent, cohabitees with children, divorcees with stepchildren, the stereotype family is the minority.

It's easy to understand, therefore, why some people rebel against the idea that Christmas, at its core, is just a straightforward family's experience. If so, I wonder where Jesus would have gone for Christmas? A single man with no children, he had rather difficult relationships with his brothers and sisters. He was a travelling preacher living with his closest disciples. But we know that there were thousands of homes where he would have been made welcome – often unfashionable, disregarded people,

people to whom he had given back their lives, with body and mind restored, people who had learnt from him the truth of the Kingdom of God; he said that they were his brothers, sisters, fathers and mothers. We are told that Christmas is above all a family occasion, and for many it is; but the religious heart of the matter celebrates the coming of the Saviour of the world. He changes everything. From him we learn that we are not just a haphazard lump of DNA riding on a piece of shrapnel called earth – we're here for a purpose. We have the capacity for deep rewarding relationships. We are loved by our Creator and can love in return. No one is excluded, no single person, no black or white, rich or poor, no stepchild, no childless couple, no widow or widower, no gay or straight. God is ready to come through every door that's opened.

This Christmas, if it finds you happy or sad, with your family or alone, God waits patiently at every door. I believe that, because he came to me, alone in a graveyard looking at the stars on a frosty Christmas night. He spoke to my hungry soul. We don't need family qualifications to put Christ back into our Christmas. All we need is to find time quietly to go to the door and open it.

'IT'S FUN BEING BAD'

24 May 1996

An eleven-year-old boy was convicted yesterday of manslaughter. He has described how he pushed off a tower block a concrete slab which tragically killed an elderly lady passing below. He said, 'It's fun being bad. It's no fun being good.' I was reminded of his words when meeting a group of young men undergoing treatment for drug and alcohol addiction in an impressive clinic near Bristol. The rehabilitation programme includes group work, mutual support and exercises in self-understanding. 'Why,' I asked, 'did you get involved in drugs in the first place?' Some said, 'To escape our problems'; some, 'To show we were one of the lads'; but the most common cause was 'boredom'. Drugs and alcohol brought a bit of daring and excitement into their lives. They enjoyed the forbidden danger. But they're not enjoying it now. They've had friends die from it. Almost without exception they desperately wanted to be free of its vice-like grip. In treatment they are supported by others who have been through it all and they begin to discover again the person they could be. But how can they sustain the fight when they're back in the world without a job or a decent home? They're afraid the 'deceiver' will seduce them back into the abyss. They tremble on the edge.

We all know that doing wrong can look hellishly attractive; and conversely, if we resist temptation it does not always bring joy, but can bring a sense of loss or resentment, and virtue is often made so unattractive, implying a lack of freedom, an absence of daring, a straitjacket.

We must offer the young people on our estates, in towns and villages the opportunity to prove themselves, to experience real comradeship in a good purpose. They have to learn that love, truth, courage, bring satisfaction so that they will choose the good rather than the wrong which only flatters to deceive and can lead to self-destruction. It takes a lot to develop the inner sense to work out what we really want from our lives and pursue it. The young, especially, need support from their community, and major commitment from adults to achieve it.

Mind you, as I rapidly approach the big sixty I still feel I have a lot in common with the youngsters I met and I also realize just how much I depend on the love of God to strengthen what is good in me. This Sunday is Whitsunday, when Christians celebrate God's promise of the Spirit – the power we can call alongside us in the battle to be good.

GIVE THE CHILDREN THEIR CHILDHOOD

7 June 1996

In our society we try to protect our children from the wrong sort of TV programmes, yet some of the most terrifying sights appear on the news. The reports often feature children starving, children in a class photo before a man walked into their school and gunned many of them down, or children who themselves have been violent. I wonder what impact these images of childhood have on children watching. We often talk about teenage idols, but what about the under-tens – who do they identify with, what sort of children do they expect to be?

Can you remember what it was like to be eight? I'm sure I had a clear image of what it was like to be a child. I wore a cap and grey jacket and shorts. I was expected to respect adults who totally ruled my world. I was a bit scared of a bigger boy who bullied me, of one teacher, and an old lady down our road whom we thought was a witch and sympathized with Germans.

But most of my memories, against the background of a distant world war, were sunny, and all my thoughts of mum and dad are warm and clear. I might argue or sulk, but I knew they were boss. I don't remember any moment of violence except dad killing a chicken for Christmas. The adults set the clear boundaries of my world – they were benevolent and I was pretty safe. Although my family was not religious we used to sing carols at school which gave us the icon of Jesus – the ideal child. 'Jesus good above all other, gentle child of gentle mother.' I remember being told the story about Jesus as a child, being firmly told off for getting separated from his mother and father. Even though as teenagers we soon discovered that the world was not quite as secure as we thought, I believe the relative innocence of childhood was a blessing.

The Bible makes the boundaries clear – the adults are in control. 'Honour your father and mother.' But the adults themselves have to be honourable – 'Do not goad your children to resentment.'

I think we need now to convey to the children of our society a clearer image of what it is to be a child. They need to know that they are safe within the adult authority, that they are free to express themselves within quite clearly defined boundaries; above all, that they are loved by their parents and by God. Sadly, they won't get this picture from most of the news – nor, indeed, from much of the adult world around them. With all the changes and brokenness in society and family life, we all have to find a way of giving the children back their childhood.

THE HOLINESS OF GOD

14 June 1996

In the Sinai peninsula is the Mount of Moses, and nearby the sixth-century monastery of St Catherine. The Bible tells us that during the exodus the people of Israel camped there in the wilderness.

Today in London, Prince Charles will launch a foundation to support the monastery, where Greek Orthodox monks still live a life of prayer. It's easier now to visit, and the monks are overwhelmed by the task of conserving this precious jewel in the history of the human/divine encounter. But it's not just the history, the ancient manuscripts and icons which make it priceless; it's also that other commodity which the market doesn't register, the holiness factor.

The prophet Muhammad is said to have visited and given it a letter of protection. People have prayed there for twenty-five centuries and more. The mountain is sacred to Muslims, Jews and Christians, a reminder to the divided world that the three great faiths have roots in common.

It was there Moses encountered the presence of God. The whole goodness of God passed close to him. He had seen the burning bush and received the ten commandments. The Gate of Heaven opened and Moses' face shone, reflecting the radiant light of God, and the world changed.

Our world is in many ways a wilderness not unlike the wilderness of the ancient people of Israel. Their lives were full of doubt, fear and cynicism. They too had a sense of foreboding; they too turned away from faith in the invisible God to more comforting idols – the golden calf on which they fixed their hopes and dreams. Sinai is a reminder to us of the holiness of God; it calls us to pray, to draw close to God, to wait for the whole goodness of God to draw near to us, to invade and radiate our soul. The mountain and the monastery are not a museum of a dying faith, but a witness through continuous prayer to the invisible God.

Sinai can awaken in us the vision of the holiness of God in our own contemporary world – the sun streaming in through the church window, the gannets diving in the storm, a great congregation raising the cathedral roof with praise to the holiest in the height, the person in the wheelchair laughing and loving in adversity, individuals at prayer, communing with God, like the monks at Sinai. Holy things, holy places, holy people are never far from us if we have eyes to see them.

TONY ADAMS, CAPTAIN OF ENGLAND

17 September 1996

As we watched Tony Adams lead the England football team to the semi-final of Euro '96 with such passion and skill, not many of us knew about his own intense personal battle. At the weekend he took the brave step of facing up to the sombre fact that he's an alcoholic. Standing before the cameras looking gaunt and vulnerable, he nevertheless displayed his strength of purpose and his human dignity.

As he finished his statement he climbed into his car and the paparazzi hounded him, offering large sums of money for his story – as so often, trying to prostitute a personal human struggle. Tony Adams said as he drove off: 'This is not about money – it's about me.' The parting shot hit the target. Not only Arsenal but many of us who also follow football and admire him will hope he climbs the mountain ahead of him.

No doubt Alcoholics Anonymous will help him discover the power outside himself, and can give him the spiritual strength to tackle the temptation to see drink as a false comforter: an alluring way to cope with stress by trying to escape harsh realities; but first of all to be honest about the situation, and then, with others, to discover a different spirit.

His words to me seem relevant to our society. Obviously some politicians believe that it is, above all, money to which we are bound. That's where the votes are thought to be in 'UK Limited'. Even the aim to raise the standard of living usually means simply to raise the amount of money each person has. Of course money is important and poverty is crippling, but a society which invests itself totally in it will become owned by it – as Jesus said, 'Where your treasure is, there will your heart be also.'

So much that is wrong with our society is not about money, it's about what's going on inside us. Our lack of respect for each other, our rage and spite, our sectional self-interest, our broken marriages, the abuse of children, the lawlessness, happen at every level of society and we can always find someone to blame, and we tend to think that money will be the answer – our comfort and the source of our strength. The more I listen to this love of money being pandered to, the more I reckon we have to rediscover the spiritual resources which are needed to bring about fundamental change. We need to examine society and see ourselves as we are, and then recognize that in many areas of our lives it's not about money, it's about us. Thank God, just as the former England captain has taken responsibility for himself and seen that his problem is within, I meet more and more people who recognize that the way to healing lies in the Spirit of God.

THE MALE SWAN-SONG

1 October 1996

A very traditional battle of the sexes has been going on outside our kitchen window this summer between Ricky and Glinty, our two swans on the moat at the Bishop's Palace. Ricky was so proud when Glinty laid her nine eggs, but then so miffed when she sat on them immovably for thirty-seven days. He was desperate, lonely and neglected. His only consolation was a swan – just like himself – that he could see reflected in the window of the summer house. He kissed this perfect, ever-available partner and tried to open the door to get in. He only returned to the nest when the first cygnet hatched and once again he became the proud father, guarding his new family with his best hissing and flapping. But then the cygnets bonded immediately with Glinty – even riding on her superb duvet – and Ricky returned to the summer house.

I may mock this old-fashioned male disorientation, but I have to admit that, from time to time I've found the massive changes in gender role rather threatening. It's hard, for instance, as a man, being identified with scenes of men behaving badly round the world, as we see so much of the inherited male role model superseded. The male backlash is no joke. Many men are afraid of what will happen if women gain more status and power. This fear is often reinforced and justified by tradition and religion.

In Africa, it is the women who are most easily infected with HIV, and the refusal to talk about AIDS, under the pressures of taboo and male supremacy, is fatal for many women and children.

And if the first reports are accurate, the new Taliban rulers in Kabul have made it clear that the policy to educate and employ women will be reversed and they will be returned to the home and seclusion of their lives. So much potential and fulfilment will be crushed and once again it will be the women in our world who will pay the price.

Domination is not the way to human happiness for men or women, and violent repressive male reaction to the progress of women only aggravates some of the world's most serious problems.

Although St Paul, as a man of his own society and generation, believed in the authority of the husband in marriage over his wife, a view which to many of us is now unacceptable, he also gave us a vision of a more blessed complementarity in Christ – 'When we have put on Christ as a garment,' he said, 'there will be no such thing as male and female – for all will be equally children of God.'

OVERWHELMING INSTINCTS

10 December 1996

There are few experiences which lead me quicker to short, sharp prayer than my horse bolting. I've even amended a line from a psalm, 'With the help of my God, I shall not jump over the wall.' It was Dick Francis, one-time Queen Mother's jockey, and Christmas-present-writer, who described the horse as a big, beautiful animal with a tiny brain and overwhelming instincts. My horse, 'Bear', fits the description. A flapping dustbin bag, air-brakes on a lorry, even roadsigns can become monsters which panic him into flight towards home.

It's comforting to think that we humans have larger brains and more control. But then I'm not so sure. Our strong feelings often represent our subconscious instincts and they are a powerful band – such as herd, tribe, race, sex, aggression and defence.

They can make us panic, overwhelming our thought control. Of course instincts and emotions are often good and indeed essential to our survival. Our sexual instincts may lead us to ruin but are also a lifeline to love and deeper vision.

Our appreciation of music may in part be intellectual, but much will come from our deepest roots as human beings – body and spirit as well as mind.

It's unwise to underestimate the part that human instincts and emotions play in the events that mould our national life. For instance, our continuous lurches over Europe seem to have more to do with instinctive feelings than reasoned responses to the problems and opportunities that Europe presents.

Panic describes the flight of a horse, and panic was the word repeatedly used to describe the selling of shares on the Stock Exchange on Friday. Perhaps a case of the flight instinct of a herd. We shall see today if good sense has reasserted itself.

Faith is the opposite of panic. It can convert fear into trust. Faith is made up of a powerful mixture of rational thinking and something beyond. It penetrates into the non-rational sources of our feelings. This is why it's so important and why religion has such power to change people – hopefully for the better, but sometimes for worse. When a person worships, it's not just an activity of the mind, but it's in the gut; it involves powerful feelings which represent, at the subconscious instinctive level, our creative origins in God.

Note. After this 'Thought' I was told that a horse's brain is big, but it uses all its mental resources sorting out its legs!

LACRIMAE RERUM –
THE TEARS OF THINGS

16 December 1996

I don't often cry watching television – it's rather a cold medium – but I did during *Casualty* on Saturday. One story-line was about a young priest who, compared with many portrayals of priests on television, was normal and good at his job. We saw him first producing a Nativity play in which his much-loved small niece was playing the innkeeper's wife. Then we witnessed an horrendous drink-driving accident in which the small girl was smashed up against a wall and killed. The priest was asked to identify the child's body. He was a mixture of professional hospital visitor and desperate devastated uncle of a favourite child. Sometimes he coped with his feelings, at others he lost control, cried out and even attacked the drunk driver.

I remember, when I was a young priest, someone gave me a slip of paper and on it were written the words *lacrimae rerum* – 'the tears of things'.

My tears were not just for the characters on the television, but because of memories of so many griefs observed through thirty years. The times when I, like others, have found it hard, if not impossible, to hold on to my professional role when grief has been overwhelming. Then I thought about the people whose profession confronts them all the time with such grief – the ambulance men and women, the military in war, the police called to road accidents, the staff of casualty departments, GPs who have to pronounce death sentences to people they have loved and cared for, for many years. Yet it all has to be professionally done. Only relatively recently has the trauma involved in such care been taken really seriously, and counselling provided when it's needed. Although it's a help to express the feelings and try to understand them, the stark reality of such tragedy presents us all with unanswered questions – and the desire to blame and punish, find somewhere to put our anger.

But as you stand by the bed or comfort the bereaved or face your own tragedy, there seems to be no reason, no sense, in what has happened. We live in a dangerous and risky world. But at least the beginnings of an answer are in the Nativity play the priest was producing. The Christian faith sees in that baby, God from God, light from light – the creator of the world intimately involved in the suffering, ultimately dying on the cross. It's not an answer which wipes away all tears in a moment, or cancels out the experience, but one which gives birth to hope and a flickering light in the darkness of the tears of things.

GOD IN A CHRISTMAS PUDDING

23 December 1996

Nothing's going to get me down today. Although we keep on being told there's not much Christmas spirit about, I've been privileged to find some in what might seem surprising places.

First, I took part in a carol service at a school for children with special needs. There were wheelchairs turned into donkeys, angels with golden crowns all dressed in white and strapped into their chairs for safety, a rebellious reindeer with a comic red nose and intoxicated antlers, and a delicious Christmas pudding waving to his mum and dad, his brothers and sisters. So much care from loving staff, a joyful telling of the old, old story. To me the presence of Christ was tangible.

The other experience was in prison. Again the same old story offered and received – not by holy innocents, but by men who had played a large part in their own downfall, mostly by drug addiction, and some not even free of that plague in prison: banged up day by day with so little to hope for, even when they come out, having made reparation. They had found their Saviour in prison, and were brave enough to stand the ribbing and worse which can come to churchgoers in prison; longing and hoping for a new start to their lives; hoping to put on a concert to raise money for charity; putting on the armour of the love of God to fight their habit. And chaplains alongside the prisoners, humanizing the place, still seeing their potential when so many write them off. We sang carols like 'Come thou long-expected Jesus, born to set your people free'. There's so much there that's hard and wrong – yet in the midst of it all, generosity, faith and transformation.

It made me glad that in Christ we have a Lord who saw the value, not just in the beautiful, successful, premier league people, but in the backward and the disabled – even those in prison. A Lord who went in to feast with the people whom society wrote off. I'm thankful that the Lord was willing to be born a poor refugee, to live as a friend of sinners, and indeed to be imprisoned and executed on the cross for our sake, so that anyone who truly knows they are loved, accepted and forgiven and does not forget it, may break free of the natural order to ignore or scrag the weak, to judge and want only to punish without offering any hope of rehabilitation. For it is for the healing of the whole of humankind that compassion came down at Christmas – and God said, 'This is my beloved Son, in whom I am well pleased.'

'I BLAME THE ELECTORATE'

18 April 1997

Years ago I remember an *Any Questions?* debate on politics at election time. There were the usual complaints blaming the politicians, when Archbishop Trevor Huddleston said, 'I blame the electorate myself.' It was as though he had said something shocking, broken the rules. There was an uneasy silence.

Presumably politicians behave as they do partly because of their own convictions and partly because they want to win our confidence and approval. In the current campaign a senior politician said, 'We've gone as far as we dare to go!' So are we, the much-vaunted consumers and taxpayers, dictating the terms? Is there any space for radical solutions to be offered? It's disturbing to think that the debate may be a mirror held up to ourselves.

What sort of society does it portray? I'm grateful that in these last few days the political leaders seem to have been tackling in a more direct way their own convictions rather than just bowing to every shift of public opinion. I was trying to understand why I felt so alienated and depressed by the debate. I've heard so many people say they just turn it off – and there are another fourteen days to go. I think it's because so often our society has been portrayed as if we are only concerned about our own particular interests. This picture is weak on ideals, on compassion, on matters of justice. We seem, on the surface, to be insular in a short-sighted way, unwilling to look to the future of the wider world.

Perhaps this is the picture derived from phone-ins, opinion polls; perhaps it's what the candidates are encountering on the doorstep. Yet as a bishop, year by year, I go to every kind of institution and community, listening to children and adults whose lives have been broken, visiting nursing homes, prisons, meeting the homeless and the unemployed. I know how much there is still to be done, even here in our relatively affluent society; yet few of these tasks seem to be vote winners.

I believe we should encourage our political leaders to go on sharing their convictions, to exercise leadership by expecting quite a lot from us, because we are not just consumers, passive witnesses; we make the society we're talking about. We hope to share in shaping a better world.

Another archbishop – Desmond Tutu – said, 'Religion is as dead without its political expression as politics is dangerous without the discipline of spiritual principles.' I hope and pray that, in the campaign, the mirror will reflect a just and human electorate.

TOUCHING THE ELEPHANT

25 April 1997

A recent Radio 4 programme deserved the equivalent of an Oscar. It was called *Touching the Elephant*. Four blind people described an elephant from what they had read or been told. It made me realize how difficult it is for people, blind since birth, to form a concept of something on the basis of words alone. They were excited and slightly nervous of what their hands were going to tell them. Under the watchful eye of the keeper they were able to explore the great creature. They were amazed at its size as they tried to reach the top, and measure the ears. Besides, the ears went down, rather than up, and the child in the party giggled as the elephant tickled her with his trunk and tried to wrap it around her. They were thrilled by the encounter. I'm sure that no sighted person could fail to have been moved by their reactions. We take so much for granted and carry in our minds so many pictures and concepts of the things we see around us.

Last Sunday, I was reminded of all this when I confirmed a young, blind woman who, after the service, asked if she could touch me. She'd heard me speak and I had laid hands on her, but she said she had no idea what a bishop looked like. So she felt round my mitre, touched my cross, held my crook and asked me to describe my robes. She seemed satisfied that my uniform was distinctive enough to be worth while. She triggered a memory of another young confirmation candidate who had just gone blind – he was dying of AIDS. I expressed my sympathy with this added suffering. He replied, 'No, it's all right. I can see what God wants me to see.'

In the exploration of God, the sighted and the blind are on a more level playing field. None of us has seen Jesus – there are no paintings or photos. After Jesus' resurrection Thomas had touched his wounds and then believed, but Jesus said, 'Blessed are those who have not seen and yet believed.' We have to form our picture of Jesus from his words, his actions and his story. But when it comes to God, we cannot see or form any picture in our minds: he is an invisible mystery. We can learn some bits about God, but the whole concept, the reality of the creator, remains beyond our reach. We can, however, in our relationship with him through prayer, experience excitement, wonder and a sense of holiness on the edge of his immensity. The ecstasy of touching the elephant sounded like the ecstasy of touching the hem of God's garment.

A BIT OF HUMAN FLOTSAM

9 May 1997

As Zaire moves closer to the climax of its rebellion, we have seen streams of refugees from Rwanda who have descended into hell. Many are still far from home, trapped by violence and fear, living out, in bone and a little flesh, the nightmare of two civil wars. One picture stood out. It's quite hard to penetrate our deadened senses. We see the pictures and we go on much as before. But one reached right through my defences to the gut – it showed a heaving mass of Hutu people, exhausted and emaciated but somehow still finding the energy to go on moving, go on hoping, go on existing. Some of them were packed into a lorry and suddenly we saw a naked baby passed out of the truck to those left behind. The child was just held by one arm, a little bit of flotsam in the human flood. We don't know if the receiving hand was a parent or a friend, or whether, like many children of war, this piece of flotsam had no parents, no friends. It was as if it was a dead chicken held by one leg – yet possibly the panicking people were trying their best in hell to get the child to the one person to whom it belonged, in that tide of despair.

The picture inhabits me. What can we do? We've seen it all before. In the country President Mobutu drives around in his motorcade, which we might take for granted in New York or even in London, but there looks scandalous. We mustn't lose our anger, we mustn't let our compassion ebb away as though these are just television pictures. We have to be committed to do something, to support the aid worker, to give Claire Short encouragement and not allow her ministry to be a Cinderella, left behind and ignored while we have a ball in the bright lights. There are steps we can all take.

Last Sunday I was privileged to take part in the Wessex Walk, when many young people and others walked in aid of the Save the Children Fund. As we finished our ten miles – a distance chosen to suit my lifestyle – a little lad, not more than eight, a determined child of peace, strode towards our cathedral in Wells – the finishing line. He said, 'I could walk twice this far' – quite! Couldn't we all?

MOBILE PHONE RAGE

2 July 1997

The other morning I settled into my seat on the train with an urgent wad of papers to read. Ten seats away a businessman got out his mobile phone and started ringing his colleagues one by one about their company's financial crisis. For most of two hours he had this loud penetrating conversation. He spent the whole time looking out of the window, so he never saw the virus MPR – mobile phone rage – spreading across the faces of his fellow passengers. I almost wished I had a mobile phone to ring him up and tell him what I thought, or perhaps ring whichever company it is who puts out those seductive adverts for train travel – the quiet game of chess, the gentle nap. I had fond thoughts about road works and traffic jams.

He must have been in some private world of his own, totally impervious, insensitive to the effect he was having on his fellow travellers. We are rightly protective of personal privacy and individual freedom, but there are also examples of what is claimed as privacy which in fact hurt the wider community.

How we bring up our children, for instance, we think of as totally our own affair, but what sort of parents we are has enormous influence, not only on our children, but through their behaviour on society itself. We may think that the break-up of a marriage is a private matter, but the ripples of pain affect children, family, friends and the community. The person who smokes doesn't only risk his or her own health, but may involve others in passive smoking, cause them long-term grief, and charge the State with sustained health care. Our private behaviour can have more knock-on effects than we imagine; our anger, our envy, our lust, as well as our aerosols, our use of our cars, can pollute the communal atmosphere.

Sometimes it's claimed that religion is just a private matter. It must, of course, be a personal belief, but all the main faiths demand a strong responsibility to the community we belong to. We are not just individuals, but rather persons in relationship. St Paul said, 'Each of us must consider his neighbour and think what is good and will build up the common life.' We are made by God for freedom, but not in such a way as to infringe the freedom of others.

Although mobile phones are very helpful technology, their intrusion into the space of others does not build up the common life.

'TILL DEATH US DO PART'

16 July 1997

During the review of the newspapers we heard mention of Alf Garnett who has for years presented us with a melancholy commentary on those familiar words from the marriage service, 'Till death us do part'. We've seen there a man and woman locked in mortal combat. We laugh at their rows, their sniping and humiliating. With them, as someone said, 'Matrimony is not a word, it's a sentence.'

We live in a society where many marriages fall apart, where many don't marry because they're afraid of committing themselves to a permanent relationship which might become a prison. It was therefore a delight yesterday to see the Queen and Prince Philip with four thousand couples celebrating their Golden Weddings. It was encouraging to see lifelong commitment as something to celebrate – as a blessing, not a curse. It can almost seem counter-culture to believe in it.

A marriage which works does not imprison or diminish the identity of each partner: it strives to enable the distinctive character of the two people to thrive by mutual encouragement. It should not leave them frustrated and lonely but, in developing intimacy, grow to a level where the two become not just one flesh, but one in spirit which survives and deepens as the flames of passion quieten. Husband and wife, as lifelong friends, carry a shared history of fun, struggles, joy and pain. They know most of each other's story and are not alone in their remembering. If they have children they have the satisfaction, by their continuing love, of providing a security which encourages the next generation to adventure. If they have no children, they can give out so much love in other ways.

Of course I know how many scars and bleak times can be involved but, if tackled and borne together, even they can become part of the whole – as can the care they may have to give each other long term, in a covenant made for better, for worse, in sickness and in health.

Maybe we need to be reminded of what marriage can be if we prepare for it, stick at it, have regular MOTs, keep no score of wrongs, and end up like a gnarled old beloved tree, grown by mutual reverence and love, which death will part, but not extinguish, before it's revived by the greater love of God in Heaven.

CLONING THE SOUL?

15 October 1997

At a forty-nation summit the Council of Europe has just called for a ban on human cloning, because it is seen as a threat to human identity. It conjures up the 'brave new world'. I can see a priest standing at the font and saying, 'I baptize you James at Globalnet.co.uk. No. 1, No. 2, No. 3.'

In Jimmy McGovern's recent serial play, *The Lakes*, three young girls drown when their boat capsizes. At the church door after the Requiem Mass for the girls, one mother turns on the priest and screams, 'You never once told me I was going to see her again.' Surely, she claimed, she had the right to hear that from her priest. But he was striving to be honest because he no longer believed in that comforting idea. Death is about identity too.

Cloning would threaten our unique identity at birth, just as it is threatened by non-existence at death. Yet like that priest, there are many who believe that life after death is an illusion. They would say that we have to recognize there is no 'meeting up with loved ones in heaven', and in the modern age we should grow out of an idea that belonged to the infancy of the human race.

But I think 'identity' is all caught up with what we can make of the word 'soul'. It's a word we lose at our peril. We know it isn't a part of the body like the heart or the brain, however significant they are to life experience and character. The soul is founded on a relationship with God through his love – in the first place as his creature and then through our life – rather as human love embraces us and changes our whole self.

We know that our basic identity is conceived through a sperm and an ovum coming together, leading to the intense miracle of birth and life. We know also that we can identify a person by a fragment of their DNA. If God is able by these personal mysteries to bring us to being, it seems just as possible to me that God could bring us to new birth in Heaven. As Jesus taught, 'In my father's house are many rooms. I go to prepare a place for you.'

I do hope Heaven won't be like a celestial Internet, but the amazing capacity of the Internet has encouraged me to believe that in other dimensions there is 'space' for us with God in Heaven. The Bible speaks of our being entered in the book of life where our soul is destined to be caught up in the wonder of the love of God – not as clone or e-mail address, but in our full identity.

ROAD TRAFFIC ACCIDENT?

18 November 1997

Under the shadow of the tragedy at Luxore I had been thinking about a continuing tragedy day by day in this country – what are known as RTAs, road traffic accidents, in which 3,600 people died last year and hundreds of thousands were injured.

Someone wrote me a letter rebuking me for using the word 'accident'. He pointed out that we talk about plane or train crashes and claimed that the repeated use of the word 'accident' suggests that it's just something that happens to us, which is unavoidable and no one is to blame. In this way he says it undermines our recognition of moral responsibility.

When I first read the letter I thought: the police always try to establish the cause and we are all familiar with expressions like dangerous driving and drink driving, and even manslaughter charges to strengthen the moral imperative. And besides, there are crashes which are nobody's fault, but it's quite difficult to identify any which don't involve some serious irresponsibility somewhere. Motorway pile-ups are not due to the fog, but to people driving too fast and too close in the fog. The tyre-burst may be the result of negligence, or, as we've just heard, the accident may even be caused by a person with a mobile phone in one hand and an order book in the other, driving with his or her knees. But surely, I thought, for an innocent victim it must be an accident. One of the constant themes, however, of _Casualty_ is that behind so many crashes there's a whole story of people taking risks, failing to observe safety precautions, rows in families, stress in business, tiredness and lack of concentration. We can see the RTA coming long before the impact, because of what someone is doing wrong to set up the situation. After all, we don't talk of the victim of a crime as being involved in an accident.

This is a tough doctrine because often the people responsible are themselves victims of the crash and face a lifetime of trauma, injury, bereavement and guilt. And we all have enough near-misses to feel 'There, but for the grace of God, go I.' However, it still doesn't change the fact that 'accident' can be a dangerous euphemism.

But where does God come into all this? He has to take responsibility for what insurers call 'Acts of God' – flood, avalanche, hurricane and the rest; but he offers us too the possibility on earth of freedom and responsibility with all the risks involved. He calls us to face up to our wrongdoing and learn to put it right. Perhaps he's using all the police film of crazy and careless driving, the campaigns for road safety, to teach us that an RTA is not really an accident but a crash caused in part by someone's irresponsibility. It could be ours.

REMAND RESCUE

25 November 1997

A fifteen-year-old boy awoke in his cell in prison to find his cell-mate hanging from the window by a noose. He supported him until prison officers came and cut him down. The boy had to go to hospital for a week to cope with the trauma.

This incident was described at the launch yesterday of the Children's Society project called Remand Rescue. This work concentrates on finding alternatives to imprisonment for fifteen- and sixteen-year-olds while awaiting trial. Many have been abused, rejected, have no stable home and are addicted to drugs. Though not convicted of any offence, these children are locked up in bad company with a high risk of contamination, bullying, violence and self-harm.

As a society we sometimes turn victims into villains even at a young age. This happens in many places in the world. We are familiar with expressions such as child prostitutes, child labour, child soldiers, street children and child pornography. Even in this country we see an ambivalence. As individuals and organizations we give generously to 'Children in Need', willingly pay for work with children when we see their vulnerability. But at the same time we have an increasing fear of what children can do – not just the petty crime, but also more serious adult-type crimes, even in rare cases rape and murder. In a variety of ways children must answer for those crimes. But in the face of these disturbing events we mustn't lose sight of the fact that in many cases children get into these nightmares because they are themselves first victims – defaced by adult wickedness or inadequacy, forced into being streetwise, stained, demoralized, amoralized, long before they reach adulthood. Yet they are precious to God, born in his image; but the reflection becomes distorted and vandalized.

The danger is that the frontiers of childhood are pushed further and further back. I sometimes think that what children are most in need of is childhood itself. I believe, if we stick resolutely to treating children up to sixteen as children, we may not be able to redeem those who have put themselves beyond reach; but with many others, we shall with proper justice, support and encouragement restore the potential God gave them.

I was impressed recently when visiting our Somerset Probation Service to hear four young people explain how, by such treatment, they had begun to mend the damage and heal the wounds and find a road back towards constructive adulthood. As Jesus said, 'Anything you did for one of the least of these my brothers and sisters, you did for me.'

ORPHAN EPIDEMIC

2 December 1997

In an African hospital, I was talking into a TV camera and I stepped back onto a dead man. He was young and had just died, but there was nowhere else to put him. The ward was full of young men dying. They mostly had wives and families. Later I went out into their villages and visited a young woman in her hut, dying against the wall in the dark, lit only by the fire where her old mother was cooking a little food for her six grandchildren. Soon she would have to look after them all. This year 2.3 million people have died of AIDS, there are 16,000 new infections each day – one in every ten is a child. Yesterday – World AIDS Day – reminded us that this is also an orphan epidemic. Nine million children have lost their mothers.

I know this is a heavy topic as you're driving to work, or having breakfast, or even a lie-in. But that's the point in a way. This world tragedy must intrude on our comfort. At home here in the UK some progress has been made by prevention, by education, by expensive drug routines. The number of deaths has been reduced by twenty-nine per cent this year. But we cannot be complacent here, and whatever happens we mustn't feel that the rest of the world is nothing to do with us. As with global warming, this world epidemic has to be tackled by all the nations, and indeed all of us playing our part. Our comfort will be short term if we opt out of the solutions – if we don't, as the Prayer Book says, 'hallow and direct our natural instincts aright' – or if we continue to defend our vested interests.

The Ugandan Commissioner for Health says, 'There is a window of hope between the ages of five and eighteen – if that group can be educated, if their behaviour is changed . . . I think we have a future.'

But it's our behaviour too. These are global questions – without frontiers.

I believe there is hope, if we find the will to act. God did not make the earth for AIDS. He also set this planet in a miraculous relationship with the sun and the stars. He gave us guidance as to how we should live in it. God is still the same God, always calling us to the good life and repentance. He listens to our prayers, he honours people who work for the suffering and for change. As soon as he sees the world united in its determination to tackle the issues, the energy and love of the creator will flow to heal and mend what we have broken.

KYOTO – GOD NOT INVITED!

9 December 1997

As we've just heard, American Vice President Gore's visit to the conference on global warming at Kyoto seems to have had little effect. Europe had been asking for fifteen per cent reductions in emissions of greenhouse gases. He offered more 'flexible' negotiation. John Prescott says this is the crossroads – 'It's time for the political science to take over from the real science and for the horse trading to begin.' One of the speakers said his island home would disappear under a deluge of biblical proportions if nothing was done. Meanwhile the political bargaining goes on – the talk about quota buying and selling and planting new forests, timing and enforcement.

I wondered what the conversation would be like if God was at the conference table. At first he's silent – seeing if they'll take his warnings, but then someone mentions compromise and God asks, 'Compromise with whom?'

'A compromise with other nations,' they reply.

'So,' says God, 'it's not a deal with future generations or with me!'

'No comment!'

God continues: 'You know, it was very difficult to create the Big Bang. All the potential for life on earth had to be programmed into the biggest explosion ever.' God is getting enthusiastic. 'One of my problems was how to get the sun and the earth in exactly the right relationship. The sun could have become a supernova and made the earth into toast, or barren like Mars. It was such a delicate balance to give you the light, heat and power, and yet at the same time preserve the earth from danger and give a chance for rational life to thrive in this beautiful paradise of a planet.'

As the prophet Isaiah put it: 'God stretched out the skies like a curtain, spread them out like a tent to dwell in.' Now we've even managed to make holes in the tent itself.

But the resistance goes on: 'The trouble with you, God, is you're not accountable to anyone. If you were, you'd know what the electorate want. There are sound reasons for not doing any more. There's our industry, our multinational corporations, our lifestyle – it would be political suicide. The people want to have total freedom to use their cars, they like life as it is.'

'But,' says God, 'I thought it was the task of politicians to lead, to explain the reality and persuade the people to support the policy which will preserve the earth and life on it for future generations.'

'Now, God, that's a bit extreme. No wonder you didn't even get a seat at the conference!'

HUMANOID GOD

4 March 1998

If, nearly three millennia ago, you walked on the beautiful green island of Delos, you would have been amazed by the great shrine of Apollo. It was reputed to have been his birthplace, and one of its spectacular features was a colossal human figure of the god himself dominating the scene. If you walk there now there are a few pieces of that colossus remaining among the ruins of the shrine.

It was this scene which came to my mind when I saw the design of the massive humanoid figure which will dominate us as we enter the Dome. The Apollo statue was plainly male, whereas at the end of the second millennium of Christ the figure is – dare I say – politically careful.

As I pondered the picture of the figure with the minute visitors passing by, or examining its innards, I couldn't resist the thought that this too – subliminally – is a god. Just as the Lottery from the beginning has toyed with divine images in its advertising, so now, not surprisingly, a vast, awesome humanoid god has emerged from the creative subconscious. I wonder if it is a spiritual parable of our age.

Yet day by day we are deluged with pictures of the flawed nature of humankind. Though we are capable of breathtaking technology, though we can be imaginative, creative, visionary and loving, we can also be cruel, destructive, snide, greedy, lustful and violent. We've done more damage to our planet than any other species and we still indulge in war and injustice. It's only too easy to understand the psalmist's heartfelt question to God – 'What is man that thou art mindful of him?' But the psalmist also recognizes the divine image in the human being: 'You have made him little less than God – made him master over all that you have made.' This puts us in perspective, commits us to a life based in prayer. Yes, we have a vocation to fulfil our human potential, love justice and our neighbour, but the age-old lesson has to be learnt again – we are not God. We make so many decisions as though we were.

It's arguable that Apollo ended in ruins because the gods were portrayed in such human terms, whereas Christ in all his humanity was not a colossus and pointed to his God and Father beyond our human definition and limitation. He didn't claim equality with God. I wonder, when I finally stand within the giant humanoid, what I shall feel. But at least there'll be one question: 'What'll they do with this when they've finished with it?'

DISFIGUREMENT AND INNER LOVELINESS

11 March 1998

I was impressed yesterday by hearing of the courage of a remarkable woman. In July 1996 Beverley Hammett was baby-sitting when the doorbell rang. She went to the door and a man threw nitric acid at her, causing terrible burns to her face and body, and she had to be put on a life support system.

In her journey to recovery, she's already had eight operations to rebuild her face. But what has been even more remarkable is the way she has been rebuilding her life. She is quoted as saying some striking words about the experience: 'I've gained a great deal from what has happened. I'm a more confident and positive person. It's made me realize we should not be quick to judge others. I believe things happen for a reason, and this is no exception.' The police, the doctors, her family and friends have paid tribute to her courage and total lack of bitterness – no cries of 'Why me?'

Beverley may be disfigured on the outside, but inside she is beautiful. She has managed by her prodigious spirit to turn a tragic event into a victory. Now she's continuing her training to be a nursery nurse.

Whether we are disfigured in our inward or outer selves, people like Beverley are an inspiration. It's only too easy to sink into depression or anger about what we've lost – or what others can be or do, that we cannot. When the damage is done by crime or negligence it can corrode us even more, and bitterness can grow all our days. But although the pain and despair can be great, it can become the raw material of loving – to be able to sympathize with others who suffer, to free others from self-pity, even to shine as a light in the world. What survives the grave is not our physical beauty but our inner loveliness, not our external wealth but our riches of spirit. No one who's healthy would choose to be disfigured, but once received, it can be transformed in a life-affirming way.

I'm reminded of those words in the Old Testament, 'By his wounds we are healed' – or St Paul's admission that he had a thorn in the flesh which protected him from pride. It's so often in battling with the scars and thorns in the darkness that the courage and spiritual beauty of the human being are most revealed. Jesus showed us that, in our struggle with our disfigurement, we are most intimate with God – even if we feel God-forsaken.

A PROSTITUTED CHILD

18 March 1998

There's an ancient Chinese proverb, 'You cannot reason with a small child, until it can carry a bowl of rice water without spilling it.' It was quoted in tributes to Dr Spock, who has just died. He was the author of a famous book on child-rearing which was next to the Bible on our bookshelf when we were struggling with parenthood. Dr Spock believed a child would learn when it was ready. With proper love and cuddles it would grow up to be responsible. Later he said, 'I've come to realize that a lot of problems are because of a dearth of spiritual values.'

Yesterday, while the House of Commons was dealing with the Budget, the House of Lords was debating the Crime and Disorder Bill and grappling with the question, 'When can a child be deemed to be criminally responsible?'

Thank God many children still grow up in a loving home, but as Chairman of the Children's Society I know many do not. One such girl aged twelve ran away from home to escape sustained physical abuse. In the next few years she began to harm herself. She began sleeping rough and a man offered her protection. He was a pimp. She was sixteen and terrified. He would lock her up and abuse her if she didn't do what he wanted. She was trapped in a life of prostitution.

She'd always been a victim of violence, never knowing security or respect. To society she's a prostitute – not a child living a nightmare. What she's doing is wrong, but the criminals are the pimps and the users. Yet it's unlikely they'll ever be charged, though some police authorities are beginning to treat their crimes as child abuse.

How far her life and situation are from the upbringing advised by Dr Spock. Yet she too is one of God's children – damaged, lost, unprotected – who in the end just disappeared. Her parents shared the responsibility: society too; her pimp and her clients were criminally responsible, but she had hardly ever known the chance to carry a bowl of rice water without spilling it, or to grow naturally towards womanhood.

Jesus was once brought a woman accused of committing adultery. Yes, he told her to sin no more, but he also judged the men who planned to stone her to death: 'Let him that is without sin cast the first stone.' How much more would he have been merciful if the woman had been an abused child. We have to tackle increased child prostitution in a new way if we are going to be a responsible society.

THE FULL MONTY

25 March 1998

It's sometimes rather embarrassing when my wife and I go to our local cinema and are recognized. For instance, should the bishop have laughed at *The Full Monty*, which, as you know, is partly about male strippers – or should he be sitting there tut-tutting his way through the moral minefield? I have to say that if my role banned warm, compassionate, non-cynical, non-lascivious laughter, I'd change my job!

Although it was expected that so many Oscars would be awarded to *Titanic* – however vast, costly and expert it is – my vote goes to *The Full Monty*, the story of the redundant workers who created hope out of their despair. One of them was rescued from a suicide attempt, another was impotent with his wife, another was so ashamed he pretended to be still at work, and another full of frustrated rage at being written off while still young and vigorous and longing to be a hero for his son.

These themes of impotence and inadequacy, the loss of the breadwinner's respect, are the real-life thorns of despair for many today. They reflect too the shame of others – old and young – who feel rejected and have a low self-image.

The men in the film, by imagination, ingenuity and daring, cross through several emotional barriers, build together their new idea and, by their guts and determination, rediscover their self-belief. They recover from the juggernaut of unemployment which laid them waste and, by giving entertainment, sent us home chuckling and more hopeful.

I agree that 'stripping' is hardly ideal employment, but that's not the point. The story for me represents one of the fundamental meanings of the faith I learnt from Jesus Christ. He offers hope to all those excluded from the mainstream – dare I say, resurrection hope. That's where God began Christ's saving work, right in the deaths of human experience. Jesus gave the chance of new life to so many of the characters he met – the rediscovery of their self-respect and, through being loved and accepted by God, enabled them to experience their worth and express it.

So I say three cheers for *The Full Monty*. It may have only one Oscar against the eleven for *Titanic*. But in the end the vast unsinkable ship sank, and for me small is beautiful, and there's no story so touching or thrilling as the restoration of life to those experiencing defeat and despair. My Oscar goes to them.

SIMULATED RACEHORSE

10 June 1998

Recently, at the Bath and West Show, I was tempted by my enthusiasm for racing and riding to have a go on a simulated racehorse. There aren't many jockeys who are six feet, two inches, weigh fifteen stone and are perilously close to sixty-two years old. It was made all the more exciting as Richard Pitman did the commentary. The horse lacked the subtlety of a real one, and after I'd ridden the Derby distance I felt I was in heart attack territory. The operator was a gent, however, and brought it quietly to a halt. I tried to dismount with dignity but, like breath, it was in short supply. I thought, 'Why don't you act your age?' Dizzy though I was, my answer came back in a flash: 'There's life in the old dog yet!'

According to the psalmist, God gave us a span of life 'three score years and ten – or if we have the strength, four score.' He teaches us to 'number our days and apply our heart to wisdom'. It's sensible advice, but sometimes people are too cautious and shut up shop on life too soon, whereas those who retain their interest, or take up new challenges, or are willing to take a few risks to live life to the full, seem to stay young at heart. I admire the remarkable people who run the marathon at three score and ten, or go on *Blind Date* at four score! Even Bob Hope, when recently pronounced dead, appeared in public to deny it and said his only regret was missing a day on the golf course.

One of the difficulties I find as I grow older is that inside I still feel like a mixture of the person I've always been – it's just that my body can't keep up with my aspirations.

Part of the answer is not to be afraid of letting go of the physical and to allow the spirit increasingly to direct our course. To keep active and interested, but accept that it's in the realm of love and the spirit that we shall find our satisfaction. Letting go can be painful, but those who are older can also gain, by learning to *be* without being hyperactive – by not being driven by faxes, mobile phones and e-mails, by having time and space to relate to family and friends, by learning to enjoy younger generations doing what we can no longer do. Above all, to ponder and pray, to think about the meaning of life, to stay close to God and his creation, and play our tune in harmony with him.

So next time I pass a simulated racehorse, I shan't try to be a jockey, but rather imagine being the horse's owner and leading it into the winner's enclosure.

STEPHEN LAWRENCE – A PERSON, NOT A TYPE

1 July 1998

The police surveillance video which was shown in the Stephen Lawrence inquiry, and the violent racial abuse by those involved, were a degrading reminder of the evil which still motivates some of our nation. They live a life which is not based on seeing other people as individuals, but as types – black, white, brown. The Nation of Islam members of the black separatist group make a similar mistake in looking for a sort of apartheid of types.

By contrast, Neville and Doreen Lawrence see Stephen, whose murder is being investigated, not just as black, but as their son; an individual they saw born and growing up, a person in his own character and right, whom they loved. Their dignity, their quiet rejection of militancy, demonstrated that their chief desire is for justice. They represent for me the good, sane people around the world who are innocent victims of thuggery, yet who want justice to be done. They have not only lost their son, but had to endure a completely changed life, submitting themselves to the public gaze in a cauldron of legal complexity and rage.

It all looks so familiar, to see the people who are striving for a good, just society subjected to the violence, the threats and counter-threats of those who refuse to see other people as anything else but a type. Not to see them as mothers, fathers, sons and daughters, as individuals with their own story and character. It is one of the fundamental steps to human maturity to see other people as human beings, with their own individuality, rather than just as religious, racial, national types.

Although in history and, sadly, today there are people and nations who call themselves Christian, who have oppressed other types of people, it's impossible to see how they can relate their behaviour to Christ himself. Over and over again he treated people as having their own soul, their own particular identity, whether they were lepers, or Samaritans, or prostitutes, or even a thief on a cross. He raised to the highest virtue in human relationships the commandment to love our neighbour as ourselves. For us the command remains, and our neighbour may be black or white, a boy like Stephen Lawrence at a bus stop, a young woman sleeping in a shop doorway, or the person next to us on the train. We can't know everyone, but we are expected to learn to see through the type to the person. This is a way of life, by which each of us in a small way can change the world – and it brings joy and hope.

HURRICANE MITCH – GOD'S SELF-LIMITATION

4 November 1998

It's estimated that as many as eight thousand people have died in Honduras and Nicaragua during Hurricane Mitch. Why do they give terrifying killers such cheerful names? As the rainwater filled the crater of the Casita volcano it overflowed and many villages were buried in flood, mud and rubble. 'It was as though the whole mountain exploded,' said one survivor. No doubt many of the people swept away to drown cried out to God, but God did not answer their prayers. And these people were poor and defenceless – just the sort of people Jesus loved. Why didn't he save them and say to the waves, 'Be still'? It couldn't be a judgement or a punishment on such innocents. It's not like Noah's flood, interpreted as a direct judgement of God. Anyone can see it's not just to punish the innocent – and God is not morally sub-human. There appear to be limits on what God can or will do. He's set the universe and the tiny earth to obey the rules by which life is possible, that essential stability which John Glenn relied on in his journey into space. Jesus himself recognized the hard reality of the scheme – 'The rain,' he said, 'falls on the just and the unjust.' The weather is no respecter of persons.

It is a global problem and we have to put away primitive ideas and look at it in a new way.

International leaders are meeting in Buenos Aires to discuss again the dangers of global warming. The brilliant scheme which enables the earth to sustain human civilization, which produces our weather and our well-being, is being damaged by our own actions. Some scientists tell us that 1998 is likely to be the hottest year of the millennium – even if it's not felt like that to us. It brings climatic changes, and we have brought it on ourselves. Some are more guilty than others. When we didn't know the cause we were not morally responsible, but now we know, we are. So great is our power that we can interfere with God's way with the weather.

Like so many great evils, the causes of global warming are made up of millions of small individual actions. Governments have to act and not just to talk, but so must we. The day of judgement is at hand. It's just claimed eight thousand lives. Nicaragua and Honduras cannot bear this alone, they need global help.

We should not despair, however, for our children and our children's children. The repeated message of the Bible is that if we repent, then God can restore. It's for us to hear the cry for help of the drowning people – God cannot do it without our co-operation.

CONSIDER THE POPPIES IN THE FIELD

11 November 1998

Today, as we know, is Armistice Day. Recently I visited a village church near Cheddar at Rodney Stoke. I was shown a stained-glass window which is a war memorial with a difference – giving thanks that all the men from the village returned home safely from the First World War. There are only thirty-two such 'thankful' villages in England, which reveals the scale of the tragedy. Meanwhile, on the front line in France, they are still unearthing unexploded shells, and their destruction echoes the eighty-year-old war. It used to be said that people would forget, but the reverse is true. Just listening to this programme over the past three days, and the television and newspaper coverage, reveal increasing interest.

Most of the new insights derive from campaigns to restore the reputation of those who have been maligned or ignored in the remembrance. The commanding officers yesterday were portrayed not as cruel, uncaring buffoons, but as good men trying to break a stalemate, and fight a war against modern artillery without modern communication. Today the Queen and the Irish President Mary McAleese will visit together a peace tower built on the Messines Ridge, south of Ypres, to commemorate Ireland's war dead, where Protestant and Catholic fought as comrades on the British side in 1917. It is sometimes forgotten that nearly fifty thousand Irish were killed between the Somme and Passchendaele.

And then, perhaps most moving of all the campaigns, to pardon those executed for cowardice. For the first time relatives were allowed to lay wreaths at the Cenotaph in their memory – some of them as young as sixteen.

In all this, like every pilgrimage, every pointing to a saved name on a roll of honour, there is a restoring of the individuality of each dot, each poppy in the fields. The soldier unrecognized and unknown becomes known again – a young man, a great-grandfather, a lover, a boyhood friend. So vast a multitude, a generation of men nearly destroyed, a grief to humankind and a grief to God.

Some say it's a childish fantasy that God can care for each soul, that he knew us from the womb; yet the drive to restore to each soldier their name and character reveals a deeper instinct which will not allow any person to be obliterated, unremembered, or die without trace.

'IF MUSIC BE THE FOOD OF LOVE'

18 November 1998

I'm grateful to Sir Simon Rattle for conducting and playing this week in a concert of music which had been censored. It's detailed in a book called *Smashed-Hits*. Stalin's suppression of Shostakovich is mentioned in the same breath as Abba's 'Waterloo' and Lulu's 'Boom Bang-a-Bang' which were deemed offensive in the Gulf War. Messiaen's music was censored during the Holocaust and the Taliban appear to have forbidden all music in Kabul.

In a way it's not surprising that music is a prime target for censorship because it has the power to inspire strong feelings, to stir the will and stimulate commitment to a cause. Think of the longing for peace expressed in 'It's a Long Way to Tipperary', or in the battle against apartheid the effect of singing 'Nkosi Sikelele Africa', or the 'Last Post' at the Cenotaph, or even 'Cwm Rhondda' at Cardiff Arms Park. Music has the capacity to communicate at a level other than plain speech, to speak to the soul and exalt the spirit. What a failure of a regime if it has to ban such communication of human freedom.

Psalm 137, immortalized ironically by Boney M, expresses dramatically the heartbreak of musicians in captivity: 'By the waters of Babylon, we sat down and wept . . . How can we sing the Lord's song in a strange land?', and then that agonized cry, 'Let my tongue cleave to the roof of my mouth if I forget you, O Jerusalem'. Just as the Psalms express the soul of a Jew, so music is essential to every faith.

For Christians there's the wonderful store of hymns both ancient and modern – though in our own day it often feels as though we are singing our Lord's song in a strange land, in what I see as the persistent distortion of church life by the press, the secularizing of Sunday, the frequent attempts to undermine the Christian vision. But it's fascinating to me how people keep on singing the great hymns, and are able to express the wonder and mystery of eternal God and even the joy of Heaven without embarrassment – even at the Cup Final, or on *Songs of Praise*, and especially at Christmas. Maybe we suppose people sing 'Hark the Herald Angels Sing' because they aren't thinking about the words, but I believe it is often because in music we are able to express a yearning of the soul, which we cannot express in speaking, where our imagination has been censored by our culture.

JESUS WEPT

18 February 1999

Last week I returned from a pilgrimage to the Holy Land. The pilgrims, like millions before them, found their faith renewed and Jesus alive in a vivid way. When we came to Jerusalem we arrived in driving rain, thunder and lightning, and the dark storm created a sombre mood as we approached the scene of Jesus' final conflict.

We walked down the Mount of Olives, looking across the valley at the Holy City, to the Church of Dominus Flevit, where we remembered the scripture: 'When he came in sight of the city, he wept over it, and said "If only you had known this day the way that leads to peace! But no, it's hidden from your sight."' The church itself is designed like a tear. He would weep today too. While we were in Jerusalem, King Hussein died, and many tears were shed. He had said there would be no peace until a solution is found to the Palestinian tragedy. On our pilgrimage we had determined not just to visit Christian shrines, not just to hear Israel's story, but also to hear the Palestinian voice, and especially the Palestinian Christian voice. One priest told us how he and his mother had been driven out of their home without any belongings by soldiers in 1948 – a home they had lived in for generations. We listened to the prophetic voice of another priest who described the gravity of the situation, their struggle to survive as they give service through schools and hospitals and try to build bridges between alienated communities.

For there are three streams of suffering which meet in Jerusalem. Many of the Jews bring experience of the Holocaust, of dispossession, indescribable cruelty and persecution. Many of the Arabs carry personally, and pass from generation to generation, not only stories of being evicted from their ancestral homes but continuing oppression since then; and the Christian Church, which began there two millennia ago, is somehow caught both ways.

Jesus wept over Jerusalem, as he wept when his friend died, as he wept in the Garden of Gethsemane. As we knelt to pray near the bedrock in that garden, the divisions, the partisan packaged views and prejudice, the aggravation of violence and insensitive domination, made Jesus' grief so real and contemporary. As we reflected on God in Christ weeping, not only did he touch the tender spot, but in a way I can't explain his tears brought comfort and eternal hope in the dark storm. So we prayed for compassion, justice and peace in Jerusalem.

'THE CHILD NEEDS A GOOD LISTENING TO!'

4 March 1999

In an NOP poll published this week for the Children's Society, children were asked, 'What would you do if you were the mayor (always assuming a mayor had power to do something!)?' Over seventy per cent said they would want to make it less dangerous for children to walk to school, to go out on their own, and provide more local places for children to play in. In a 'Safer Routes to School' project Camden Council worked with children identifying hazards along the routes, preparing a photographic audit of the safe and the unsafe where they walk and play, and testing out the traffic-calming measures.

If you're four feet high you get a quite different view from someone who is six feet high – the six-footer may see over the car parked by the zebra crossing, whereas a four-footer may have to venture out to look round it. Do you remember that poster which showed a child and the caption read, 'This child needs a good listening to'? It's one of the ironies that in spite of all the talk about the free society, there are important ways in which freedom for children has been reduced, not increased. I remember as a boy walking a mile to catch a bus to school, playing out each evening in the street, and we had places of adventure nearby where we played without fear. But now some children have to be driven to school and they don't have nearly as much freedom because of our often understandable fear of abuse, abduction and traffic – and children mind!

It's not unusual for us to leave children out of our calculations – for instance, the convenient view that children suffer less if parents, who are always arguing, divorce. Did anyone till recently ask the children what they thought?

People are so ambivalent about children – sometimes treating them like little angels, sometimes treating them like devils. But children are children. They are mostly the product, first of adults, and then of their peers, as they become themselves. Many of them are rarely listened to and have to struggle through their childhood on the edge, bearing their hardships in secrecy and fear. Do we adults really know what children are thinking and feeling? Even those who love them and care for them may not know what's really going on.

Jesus' own attitude was remarkable and encouraging. He treasured what children thought. He suggested that in some way we each have to become like a little child, because a child often has a vision uncluttered by the complexity and cynicism of the adult world. Children seem sometimes to have a clear line to God. By listening to the children we may enlighten our understanding and make the world safer for them.

BUDDHA STILL SMILED

23 September 1999

Many people will have been moved by the picture in the *Independent* yesterday of the statue of the Buddha in Wufeng near the epicentre of the earthquake in Taiwan. The huge golden figure appears to be almost untouched by the wreckage of the buildings around him, with the familiar discreet smile intact. Perhaps the first thought might be that he seems indifferent to the suffering around him, but Buddha was especially concerned with suffering. He analysed it and was highly realistic about all conscious life, inevitably experiencing it. By penetrating its causes, he showed how suffering could be transcended. Perhaps the Buddhists in Wufeng will see the escape of the statue as a sign of their vision of the truth and find some peace and security in the chaos. Because Buddhists have no god to account for, their question of suffering is about human understanding and detachment. Christians, on the other hand, have to say something to answer the question, 'How can a God of love, who is almighty, allow an earthquake twenty-five miles deep in the earth to result in the deaths of thousands of people, following the thousands who died in Turkey recently and the victims of hurricanes, floods and the so-called Acts of God?'

There are philosophical arguments. For instance, to have an earth which supports life there will inevitably be suffering; or if there is to be the possibility of freedom and goodness, there also have to be struggles, and even evil. But when the philosophy has been thought, the Christian answer to suffering is not an abstract idea, but a Gospel of an innocent man hanging on a cross by nails through his wrists and ankles, his giving of himself for humankind, his entering into the whole human mess – God immersed, God in the child beneath the rubble, God in the terrified old woman cowering under a table in a shattering building, God in the grief – and yet his name will be called Wonderful Counsellor, the Mighty God, the everlasting Father, the Prince of Peace. His reaching out to embrace the suffering has brought hope, compassion and love for the vulnerable human race.

Though Buddhism and Christianity are very different, it's encouraging that they both expect their adherents to act in compassion wherever there is suffering in the world.

NO IDENTIFIABLE REMAINS

8 October 1999

There have been so many pictures and words – the cars, once shining possessions, not collected in station car parks; a young rescue worker faced with the unfaceable asks, 'In the end who do you blame – God?'; the wounded talking about the trauma which will be a nightmare for years to come. But above all, what the papers called 'the tomb', 'the death trap' – carriage H of the 6.03 'flyer' from Cheltenham to Paddington – and in this shrouded holocaust, the horror that cannot be described.

The phrase 'no identifiable remains' haunts me; with the number of dead increasing day by day – still over one hundred and twenty to be accounted for. In spite of DNA testing and dental records, there will be unidentified ashes after cremation at one thousand degrees centigrade.

To have no body to grieve over, no familiar signs of the beloved, leaves in those left behind an aching void.

The brother of the driver from Swindon wrote on a card accompanying a bunch of flowers laid on the bridge overlooking the scene: 'My only wish is that he never suffered.' That must have some hope in it – with so great an impact, and such a fire, only a split second of conscious experience. But then there's all the unfinished business of sudden death – no goodbye, no reconciliation, no way back. All the 'if onlys', all the anger, all the loss – so hard to bear. But still that fear, 'no identifiable remains' – no answers, no comfort from a burial.

Then I thought, 'Earth to earth, ashes to ashes, dust to dust.' It's where we all end this life. Sudden death or slow – the answer of nature. But did the victims' story lead to obliteration on Tuesday 5 October – are we all eventually just earth, ashes and dust, containable in a small urn, like a leaf falling from a tree becoming earth again, or does every human being have a soul, an identity precious to God – not to be lost or wasted, a person in relationship with others?

I believe in the soul. Because we have souls, God has given us the freedom to live this dangerous life.

If I had to face the fact of 'no identifiable remains', I'd persuade all those young and old who loved the person to write their part of the story, their feelings and memories. I'd make a scrapbook with pictures of the blessed times, the fun, the love – and so reflect the spirit of the beloved, as a sort of sacrament of the soul now freed to be with God.

'PILGRIM'

8 March 2000

Today is Ash Wednesday – the beginning of Lent. At the Bishop's Palace in Wells we're blessing a new statue in the garden. It's of a man seven feet high, with a shaved head, wrapped only in a shroud. He has no possessions, no clothes, no shoes. His eyes are shut, concentrating on God. He's moving slowly forward, struggling with the human journey, yet somehow serene. He could be a monk, or Lazarus emerging from his grave, but he's called simply 'Pilgrim'.

He's been with us for several months, most of which time I've been struggling in my own small way to get fit again after illness. Whether confined to bed or home, I've had a taste of the wilderness which many people have to suffer through years of pain and loss. It can isolate you and make you feel helpless and go through a dark tunnel in your spirit.

But there have been positive sides to the confinement – all the love and prayer received, and time to think. Not a comfortable place, but perhaps a necessary one. The questions were mostly to myself. Who am I becoming? What sort of person – as Christian, husband, father, friend and colleague? To whom and to what have I given my inner self? As the years pass, our habits, our scars, our fears and desires mould the person we are becoming. Almost without noticing we stray off course and lose our way. My enforced space gave me some sharp reminders – but thank God, I rediscovered the truth with which my faith began: that even though I know my many failings, I am loved by God.

In Lent we remember Jesus' testing as he fasted in the wilderness exploring his destiny. Who was he, what was he to do? His way was to love and obey God, not to dominate people, nor glorify himself. In Lent every Christian and perhaps some non-Christians may make a space to ask themselves, 'Who am I becoming?' How can I get in touch with my soul, stifled by the relentless preoccupation with the material world? Who am I becoming in God's eyes? What's happening to my integrity, my values, my relationships, my prayers? In a way we are all pilgrims towards our destiny, exploring who we are becoming and who we could be.

TAX FOR THE COMMON GOOD

15 March 2000

Whether we agree with Mr Hague's analysis in his speech last night or not, I'm grateful that he's reminded us that taxation is a moral matter, and it's an appropriate debate before the Budget. So often taxation is spoken about simply as a matter for economic decision as though it was morally neutral. It is obviously a complex economic balancing act in hard national and world markets, trying to create wealth and assess social priorities. On the one hand there's enormous public demand for essential services to be provided, like health and education; and yet on the other, a common resentment that we have to pay the tax necessary to foot the bill.

Although taxes have been levied through the ages for many scandalous purposes, and then often squandered or wasted, there lies behind taxation, as we understand it, strong moral roots. The Old Testament prophets warned the people of Israel that they would bring God's judgement down on themselves if they did not work for a just community. This had to be achieved by fairness for rich and poor at the city gate, and also by the rich heeding the warning that accumulating wealth without caring for the poor, the alien in their midst, the widow and the orphan, would bring disaster. This was the prophetic call for corporate responsibility, in addition to their care for themselves, if there was to be a godly and stable society.

In a way, taxation involves a realistic doctrine of humankind. It's not unusual for the rich to ring-fence their wealth. In our world, great extremes of poverty and wealth coexist. Our vast, complex, international community requires us to see that the second great commandment, to love our neighbour, is not just a challenge to individuals, but a corporate goal for the sort of world we should try to build. Of course we should give individually to Mozambique and Madagascar, but the effort would be hopeless without international government contributions. We do need to learn to be responsible for each other and enable all citizens to belong, so that the poor and weak are not caught in a dependency culture, but are given the necessary support and encouragement to reach their potential, and play their full part.

Admittedly, sometimes governments use tax wrongly, but it is the democratic task to hold them accountable. We also ought to support them when they attempt to use taxes rightly and form policies which strengthen the common weal.

If we only see tax as a blow against our own well-being we'll probably resent it, but not if we recognize that it is the way in which we share in the common good.

HOLY FATHER AND HOLY CITY

22 March 2000

A Palestinian leader yesterday expressed his pleasure at the Pope's visit to the Holy Land: 'He does not treat us as children of a lesser God.' When the Pope arrived in Jerusalem last night he came as a friend of Israel and a friend of the Palestinians. He walks into a bleak history and a grim present reality in the Holy City. Even as he arrived, masked gunmen elsewhere were demonstrating that for some, on both sides, violence still seems the only way. We know that there is still injustice corrupting the peace process. How can the cycle of violence be broken when so much hate, fear and desire for revenge consume the human heart? How can people of different faiths find reconciliation when there are such deep scars, and oppression between peoples and nations?

Into this cauldron the Pope has come in his physical weakness to fulfil his dream. He calls everyone to pray for peace and unity. He comes in the spirit of penitence that he recently expressed for the wrongdoings of the Church through the ages. He comes in humility – determined not to treat Jews and Muslims as children of a lesser God. At Hebron, Christian, Jew and Muslim can pray together at Abraham's tomb. Although there are real differences, there's much in common between these three faiths and yet, sometimes because of religious conviction and sometimes because of political ambition, they have warred against each other. If we continue in this mode we shall bring large parts of the world to anarchy. It would be worth a great deal if this visit by John Paul the Second encourages all those people of faith who search for peace and justice; for without justice there can be no lasting peace.

For Christians in particular there is a huge responsibility to approach the conflict with humility and respect. So often Christian nations have acted in ways which contradict the example and the teaching of our Lord. Jesus seemed to recognize there would be wars, but said, 'Blessed are the peace makers' – who somehow manage to find bridges, break through distrust and create understanding where there has only been conflict. Jesus' teaching was and is scandalous, and 'Love your enemies' is not a popular creed, let alone 'Turn the other cheek', but the vocation of the Church is to be true to the longing for peace and the establishment of justice.

I thank God that the Pope, frail, exhausted and weak, has lived out his dream and hope that all Christians and perhaps people of all faiths will pray for the peace of Jerusalem.

FREEDOM FROM SLAVERY

29 March 2000

In the argument over the Police Foundation Report published yesterday on how we should deal with drugs, little attention was given to the question of why people take them at all. Why is it that the campaigns to say 'No' and the strict legislation have not been sufficient deterrents? Perhaps one of the answers is how much people indulge in all sorts of behaviour which may well cause them harm.

Many of us continue to over-eat or under-eat even when our health is put at risk. In spite of all the warnings, people through-out the world still smoke. Although there are signs of driving and drinking reduction, through education and deterrent, many people still drink too much and harm themselves and others. Some still engage in unsafe sex in spite of the danger and even seeing their friends die from the results. Some self-harm in the direct way with a razor.

Many of us engage in sport which we know can harm us. When I get on my horse I know the risks involved, and risk is part of the buzz which rock-climbers feel. Some risks enhance our lives but others diminish them.

Sixty people have died from taking Ecstasy in a decade, but multitudes die from cancer. Many run fatal risks through infected needles and addiction plunges many others into a life hardly worth living.

Through the years I've been saddened to see how often drugs are used to try to meet spiritual hunger which faith could satisfy. Ecstasy itself was originally described as 'an exalted state or feeling of delight and rapture', which is the way I and many others would describe some experiences of God. The Bible also warns us about the attractiveness of the forbidden fruit. Adam and Eve eat of the one forbidden tree and are plunged into guilt, and the result is exile from the garden. Why else would young-sters huddle together behind the bike-shed for a forbidden fag, if prohibition didn't increase the appeal?

The spiritual hunger becomes even clearer in the use of food, drink, drugs and nicotine to overcome the low self-image, to ease the worries, to comfort the despair. We all experience wretched times and long for relief. I learnt from the Christian faith that through the love of God each individual could find worth and affirmation, and faith can be an antidote to our worries, and the strength of prayer can help us survive and even bring victory over despair.

And, as for happiness, which we all look for; well, Jesus promised abundant life, and that's not damaging or addictive and leaves no headache or hangover in the morning.

REASON ESSENTIAL

6 May 2000

The death toll in Uganda of members of the cult of the Church of Restoration of the Ten Commandments is now over a thousand. Presumably they all knew the commandment, 'You shall not commit murder.' When we hear about such cults, it's only too easy to distance ourselves from them as an African phenomenon. But Waco and other cults in the States and Europe tell of people persuaded to believe and be enslaved by the sordid, absurd and violent.

It's alarming how often religious hopes and fears are abused, when victims become possessed beyond all reason by dominant individuals and ideas. They forfeit their own identity to the cohesive pressure of the group and the authority of their leaders.

Religion is especially vulnerable to such abuse, because it concerns the search for God, and in a sense God is unknowable and depends upon revelation. This leaves a vast space for fraught and distorted imaginations.

This is why reason and common sense have a part to play in faith. We recognize that reason cannot prove the existence of God. We know that the experience of God can take us beyond the reach of natural explanation to the realm of mystery, but God has given us brains and expects us to use them. God is not trying to entice us into madness, or suggest that his reality contradicts what is rational, even if God is immortal and invisible.

We need our reason to check what we believe, and to see how God's truth and wisdom relate to our experience – to distinguish faith from fantasy, sense from non-sense, and love from hateful illusion.

For Christians too, we have the test of what is coherent with Jesus Christ. In his name we have rejected many of the mistaken and violent perceptions of the past. We don't believe that God wanted whole cities of people banned and destroyed. We don't believe that menstruation makes women unclean, nor do we believe that a God of love would submit his children to everlasting torment, even though we have to face responsibility for the way we have lived and will face a judgement.

Reason and common sense must not be a straitjacket, or stifle our vision of God, but rather be a testing of our primal religious instinct in our search for him.

———◆———

KIDULTS

6 July 2000

Recently I was reading a fascinating story to our grandson about a mouse and a monster called Gruffalo. It was not long before our grandson, who is, after all, only five months old, became distracted by the pleasurable thought of splurting his liquidized carrot far and near! But I wanted to know how the mouse outwitted the monster. Then I heard on yesterday's programme the solemn news about kidults – an advertiser's name for adults who enjoy children's books. Some apparently even have to have their books covered in an adult way to avoid the humiliation of being a kidult. The danger is that they are really trying to escape from the grim adult world into a fantasy, anaesthetized so as not to frighten the children, where they can play in safety, where all the monsters can be defeated and the little mouse wins through in the end.

Admittedly there are dangers in habitual regression, but we all agree it's tragic when a child is deprived of its childhood – as many are in our world, as soldiers, street children, slaves and prostitutes – or even just expected to behave and carry burdens like adults before their time. But it's also serious when the child in the adult is suffocated, crushed or rejected. If we kill off the child in us we can become habitually self-important, moralistic, bossy and pompous adults, without any inkling of our own absurdity. 'The king is in his all together – he's all together as naked as the day that he was born.' The humour, the sense of fun that springs from the child within graces our lives, whereas the humour grown in the distorted, grubby and cynical corner of the adult mind can degrade us.

St Paul and Jesus give us complementary views on the subject. St Paul warns us against infantile escapism in our faith: 'When I was a child, my speech, my outlook and thoughts were childish.

When I grew up I finished with childish things.' We do have to remain firmly rooted in the adult reality of God's world. But Jesus taught that we have to become like a little child to enter the Kingdom of Heaven – a fascinating idea: perhaps rediscovering innocence, restored to a sense of wonder and, pray God, a bubbly sense of humour without which the human race is doomed. Kidults, it's time to stand up and be counted.

URBAN/RURAL UNITY

13 July 2000

Since Lord Runcie's death on Tuesday, we've heard many tributes. I shall remember him most, not for his ecclesiastical achievements, but as a warm, loving, wise, prayerful, humble and very funny human being. He was my father in God and then a friend throughout my ministry. May he rest in peace and rise in glory.

He also made big contributions to our nation. For instance, he was responsible for two substantial reports: *Faith in the City* in 1985, followed in 1990 by *Faith in the Countryside*. They contained much prophetic analysis and prescription, and they identify issues which have later developed into sore places. We hear a lot about the North/South divide, but sadly there is also some enmity between the urban and the rural.

I spent my first thirteen years as a bishop in East London and the last nearly nine years in Somerset. Attitudes are hardening at a time when the countryside, like the mines, the docks and industries, is facing serious threats and changes. *Faith in the City* tried to explain the plight of Urban Priority Areas to the suburban and rural, and *Faith in the Countryside* tried to return the compliment. But now there are examples of a dialogue of the deaf.

Yet we are one society, and we profoundly need each other. The cities need the countryside to provide lungs, space, food, drink, to help prevent urban alienation from nature, give reminders of community and by abundant beauty bring renewal of soul, recreation and stress antidotes. The countryside in turn needs the urban as a source of vibrant cosmopolitan culture, as a provider of services, like health and education, and an institutional support as well as a market, and the financing of the maintenance of conservation of the countryside itself. Cities and towns without the countryside, and the countryside without the urban, would both be deprived.

There are problems which could be solved by listening and compromise, rather than uncomprehending conflict. We have to recognize that there are varied values and ways of life and try to respect and understand them. I believe that if mutual trust could be restored then some of the conflicts could be healed.

The same Lord is immersed in both village and city – 'the earth is the Lord's and all that is in it'. It will need good sense, real listening and a readiness to compromise, to rediscover the harmony we all need, to share the blessings of both.

FASCINATING MURDER

20 July 2000

On this programme yesterday in a discussion about the tragic death of Sarah Payne, a clinical psychologist, Oliver James, had the courage to challenge us all about our apparent fascination with gruesome murder. He referred to the TV programme *Cracker*, where the unlikeable Fitz deals with the evil in the human mind. But we could add *Silent Witness, Taggart, Prime Suspect* and a thousand other murder programmes. Although the media now make such terrors more accessible, this fascination is not new – crowds have always gathered for hangings, and Tyburn fascinated for centuries. Even today motorway accidents appear to fascinate us, partly because of concern for the victims, but when does that slip into ghoulishness?

We tend now to use 'fascinate' in a positive way; we're fascinated by the Internet, or an eclipse, but the roots of the word are darker. It derives from witchcraft, like the word 'enchant', which began with the terror of being spell-bound – another word which has slipped in meaning from the terrifying to the pleasurable. Fascinate was also used of snakes who were believed to cast a spell by their look. I've seen a mink have a hypnotic effect on a duck before the kill. And so to 'fascinate' meant to enslave faculties and judgement, and rob the victim of the power to escape or resist.

This brings us to the health warning: fascination with gruesome murder, whether in fact or fiction, can, if we are vulnerable (and perhaps we all are), damage us. This is clear from copy-cat crimes, but how do we know whether the type of persistent exposure to gruesome, horrific murders in newspapers, on most evenings' television, is not, in some way (however subliminal), addictive, perverting our judgement or weakening our resistance? It all slips past, but it's there in the videos of our mind.

I asked myself too about fascination with God. There can be ambiguity there, as we see only too clearly from history that severe inhumanities have been done in God's name, and yet Christ himself was seen to be someone who freed people from 'enchantment by devils', from the fascination with horror. His loving, even from the cross, was not to deprive us of our judgement, but to empower our freedom; not to enslave our faculties, but to give abundant life; not to spell-bind us, but to release the bonds of evil.

CONCORDE –
ICON OR IDOL?

27 July 2000

I've done several 'Thoughts for the Day' following plane crashes when the central fact to be considered has been the loss of life, the nightmare of a shocking and tragic impact. But this is the first time there has been grief for the plane as well. Interviews in Bristol, where twenty-two Concordes were made, expressed the sort of shock and sadness associated with the death of a film star – and a local one at that. In France a civic leader said it had created a great emotional wave, it was the crash of a symbol of the sixties.

So much of this shows that Concorde is an icon. It touches a nerve, whether because it's like the paper darts of the school room, or the dreams of the space comics, like the *Eagle*, or its beauty of line – a pure white angel – or the sense of brilliant achievement and national pride, thought of as a thrill to ride in, an adventure of a lifetime. We've tended to forget the major problems posed by its early days. Could we afford it? Would it ever be economical? Was it ecologically sound? Even the concern about greenhouse glass being shattered. It still showed us in a better light.

What do we do with a shattered icon? Well, hopefully the cause of the crash will be found and the great birds will fly again. But we'll not easily wash away those pictures of the trailing flames, the ashes, the bodies and the scarred land.

Maybe the discovery of a frailty after all these years will help us get it in perspective – however much we still say, 'That's Concorde', looking up at the vapour trail, or hearing the super-sonic booms. We know now that the icon is vulnerable as aircraft are, one day, in one place, at one time.

Icons and Christianity go back a long way. There's part of that history which warns against the icon becoming an idol, worshipping it as if it were God. The icon's purpose is to remind us of the creator. I rejoice in the intelligence, design and manufacture of Concorde, to make peace, not war; to break through barriers; to take the human race where it had not been before at a new speed; to inspire and raise our sights; but to recognize that it too will be on the shelf as time and the human race move on to the next exploration and discovery. Yet even in the museum it will somehow grace our time.

EARTH ABUSE

1 December 2000

I notice as I get older my prejudices tend to harden – like the distress I feel when I see a group of young people smoking. I think, 'Surely they must have been taught about the damage they're doing to their beautiful God-given lungs.' Yet the peer group fellowship, the attraction of forbidden steps to adulthood, and that sinister nicotine comfort, lure them into self-destructive behaviour.

But my self-righteousness was stung by the last episode of David Attenborough's TV series *The State of the Earth* which was a prophetic judgement on the indecision at The Hague on greenhouse gas emissions, and on our self-destructive behaviour on a gigantic scale. The earth, whether you believe it was by accident or God's design, is so marvellously placed within the universe, the stars and planets, to support life, to benefit from the sun and yet be protected from it, and to sustain all the brilliant species which David Attenborough and his team bring on film into our homes.

But, like some heavy smokers, we go on fooling ourselves that 'all this global warming is overstated'. Yet the films show us endangered and dying species, lifeless, colourless coral reef, damage to so many eco-systems around the world, and leave us in no doubt about the increasing damage we are doing.

The final stark warning was Easter Island where huge stone statues remind us of a people who made their island unsustainable by felling all their trees, leaving it barren, with no more homes, no boats to go fishing and no creatures to keep the island and its people alive.

The purpose of prophecy is to change attitudes and practice, to avoid the judgement people bring on themselves. It's not just a healthy lung at risk, serious though that is, but an amazing, exquisite and, I believe, divine creation. The warnings have had some response – schemes to steward the butterflies, the seahorses, the trees, to put man back into co-operating with nature rather than destroying it. But these small steps will be swept away unless the prophecy reaches into every government boardroom, kitchen and mud hut. Noah gave his warnings too, but the people ignored them and took no action because they preferred to go on with their lives unchanged.

Perhaps we shall have more authority to object to our children smoking behind the bike-shed when the adults take more seriously our own abuse of the world's natural resources.

TWIN SOUL

8 December 2000

Yesterday the main press pictures showed the hand of a baby, known as Jodi, gripping her father's finger. Last night her parents, Mr and Mrs Attard, and the surgeons were interviewed on television to express their thoughts and feelings about the twenty-hour operation to separate Jodi from her conjoined twin

Mary, to give Jodi life when otherwise both would have died. Mrs Attard said: 'Jodi might realize that something is missing from her, so she's holding our hands much stronger.' The strange unity of the twins' birth had been broken. I so admired her parents who still see Mary as having her own identity. They had been willing to entrust the children to God even though, unseparated, they were going to die. But the court ruled otherwise, and Jodi lived and Mary died, but in faith Mary still lives with God. This faith enables them to love and accept Jodi. As one of the surgeons said, 'Mary is not a ghost but a guardian angel.'

It had been a situation full of doubt and fear – just human beings facing a problem posed by nature, leading to an almost insoluble ethical dilemma with all the possible pain and grief. Sometimes we have to decide when God's wisdom is hidden behind the cloud and we travel beyond our rules and dogma – a naked struggle of the human conscience. Some kind of faith was essential in the parents and doctors and nurses alike. They all made their best decisions in the darkness of unknowing. The professionals using their knowledge, skill and care in defence of the possible life, in a way representing society together with the parental love. I believe that this combined prayer and struggle may be as close as we can get to God's will. Jesus, after all, did say: 'Greater love has no man than this, that a man lay down his life for his friends.' Mary could not make the decision for herself, but human beings do give their lives in sacrifice and may we not think that in her eternal soul, under the merciful eye of God, she might have affirmed the decision to give her life that her sister, her other self, might be allowed to live. For Mr and Mrs Attard and all Christian people believe that God's love was never more truly shown than in the life-giving sacrifice of Christ.

NKOSI – AIDS PROPHET

12 January 2001

I'm looking at the picture of a twelve-year-old boy, in a smart suit, white shirt, tie and trainers. He's smiling and his eyes are sparkling. He's speaking to a vast gathering of adults including the President of South Africa, Thabo Mbeki. As the boy speaks, the President leaves. Perhaps because he couldn't bear to listen to the plea from one so young that people with AIDS should be treated like human beings, that the government should provide AZT to pregnant mothers, that he didn't want babies to die.

The boy who put the President right is named Nkosi. He's dying, like millions of children, women and men around the world. Nelson Mandela called him 'an icon of the struggle for life'. But why did it take an innocent child to break through the fear and guilt, the prejudice and politics which shrouded this tragedy in confusion and inaction? No one could say that Nkosi was to blame for being born with HIV. The child exposes adult hypocrisy and says things just as they are. He has shamed male-vested interests, sexual taboos and secret worlds, which have caused dangerous delays in tackling the reality of AIDS.

Sometimes I can't understand why God allows so much freedom and so much suffering. When people take risks with their lives wrongly and knowingly, they are responsible, but Nkosi represents millions of innocent victims who never had a choice. No doubt for some people it's a good enough reason not to believe in a loving God, but that's not the way it affects me.

I see Nkosi as a Christ figure. Suffering is a big part of the world's experience. But we do not believe that God is a vast impersonal creator, impervious to our cries. Rather, we have seen his love precisely in an innocent young man dying on a cross. The only way this faith can be justified is the reality of Heaven which innocent suffering demands. But Heaven is no excuse for inaction now. The world can tackle the terrifying

AIDS epidemic. As Nkosi pointed out, we have medical treatment, available now to the rich. It will cost us dear, but the cost
of not doing what we can is far greater. Nkosi has survived longer
than most of the babies born with HIV – long enough to speak
his message with such dignity and grace, because of the medical
and loving support he has received. That in itself is a sign of
hope, if only we will act internationally and individually. I shall
frame Nkosi's picture – lest I forget.

SONG THRUSH SILENCED

26 January 2001

I was delighted to hear about the Big Garden Birdwatch
launched for the RSPB by the *Today* programme yesterday.
We've got the forms from the website and we'll keep watch in
the Bishop's Palace garden at Wells. But it took me back to an
evening in spring in our own home. I remember it because the
sun was shining and I sat listening for an hour to a song thrush
singing a wonderful varied programme which no human music
could replace – even the nightingales flew away to practise.

This amazing sustained performance was probably for the
benefit of a mate, but some sentimental part of me felt it was
composed and sung for us. That day I had bought and planted
some flowers in the garden. Because the slugs always appreciate
new delicacies from the garden centre, I surrounded the plants
with protective anti-slug pellets. The following evening I sat
waiting in the hope of an encore, but there was only silence. I
comforted myself with the thought that the thrush had moved to
another garden, but there was no song thrush in the area.

It not only gave a sense of loss, but also a guilty fear that, in
return for its song, I had killed it. I felt I had been so careless.

Even if I didn't in fact silence the bird, I should have found out if what was poisonous to slugs might also be poisonous to birds, and hope to find other ways of protecting my precious plants – I think some sand would have done it.

This might all seem a bit twee, but the sorrow inside me was real. I know that birds, like all God's creatures, live in a cycle of eating and being eaten, of killing and being killed. The song thrush bashes snails to get at the flesh, the magpie steals song thrushes' eggs, the cat traps the fledglings. It's not good for humans to become alienated from the harsh realities of nature. I must say I struggle with the prodigious facts of the fight for survival, but have come to see that death and new life are inextricably bound up with each other.

So it's great that the Big Garden Birdwatch will encourage adults and children to observe and monitor and keep real about nature and learn about our human role in it. Few things are more dangerous than projecting onto animals our human thoughts and feelings. It can lead to interventionist kindness that can itself kill. The task is to revere and conserve, but to see always that without natural death there will be no natural life.

MECCA AND MURDOCH

27 April 2001

This week Sir Paddy Ashdown moved a motion for his party in the House of Commons, probably for the last time. It was a *tour de force*. In it he drew a parable from the sight in every Albanian village in Kosovo of a graveyard facing Mecca, and on every house a satellite dish, as he said, facing Murdoch. He thought that in the end Murdoch would have the greater influence. It's a startling thought and made me wonder what answer I would give about television and the Christian faith. We all live with the communication explosion, but not uncritically, not to be fooled into thinking it meets our deepest needs.

Perhaps global communication by satellite will help us to be less tribal and narrowly nationalistic; sometimes, like the World Service of the BBC, giving people a truer picture of their own conflicts as they are happening. But whose world-view are we getting? The great world faiths also span the globe and have their own families of faith to widen their horizons.

Perhaps too, global communication can broaden our understanding of the great moral issues facing our world, but then we ought to be watchful over whose values are being propounded. The faith communities all have a strong moral basis and a mostly clear set of values, and each offers a way to live which is a precious guide through the moral maze presented by the mirror which television holds up to the world. The prophets of religion often have to recall people from the ways of the world, to a vision of the holy and wholesome life.

But the greatest contrast between Murdoch's eye-view and Mecca and all the great faiths is the offer of the spirit, the relationship individuals and communities can have with God. This gives a different perspective to what it means to be human and the way we use the created earth, and the way our souls grow in prayer.

But we know too that religion also needs correction. Many of the world conflicts have a religious element as Christians and Muslims, Arabs and Jews, Catholics and Protestants continue to demonstrate. Maybe global communication could help greater mutual understanding, give opportunities to discover how much we have in common. Sometimes the arteries of religion harden, and the spirit can start to flow again when we listen to and observe and respect each other and attend to the needs of the world around us.

CONTROL FREAKS

4 May 2001

In an ancient thought, Pliny the Elder commented on the frightening medicine practised on Romans in the first century AD. 'Heaven knows,' he wrote, 'the medical profession is the only one in which anybody professing to be a physician, is at once trusted, although nowhere else is an untruth more dangerous. We pay no attention to the danger, so great for us is the seductive sweetness of wishful thinking.' If we were to study the methods of Pliny's time, we would rush out and give profound thanks for the Health Service in our own day.

Yet yesterday the National Audit Office warned that over the next ten years the NHS will face almost four billion pounds in costs for clinical negligence. This includes massive increases in claims made, the awards given and what has been called the 'compensation culture'. In our attitudes to hospitals there's an interesting television contrast between *ER* and *Casualty*. *ER* represents the American scene in emergency departments where doctors sometimes appear to be more worried about litigation than they are about taking appropriate risks for patients, whereas, although *Casualty* shows growing fear of prosecution, it's not yet so paranoid. Of course it's essential there is compensation for negligence and high standards of care and the best training possible, but I can't help feeling that medical staff are being expected to act like God, with the technology to match. There's a narrow line between proper caution and the disabling fear of mistakes and failure.

It's not only in medicine that we seem to think we can control everything, if only people would do their jobs properly. If something goes wrong there must be someone to blame, to pay the cost. It's almost as though we believe we are owed solutions for the worst that life can throw at us. Yet in many parts of the world the people experience nothing but the uncontrollable – flood, famine, war, earthquake, poverty; and it's not surprising that faith is often more alive in such places. We're thankful life is generally not like that for us, but if we have no way of dealing spiritually with the uncontrollable either in God or in ourselves, we shall always be looking for someone to blame. More important, we shall miss out on praying for our doctors and nurses as well as for ourselves, and lose the healing power or strength to cope which comes from God.

Pliny the Elder, in command of a Roman fleet, took the ships to shore to rescue the victims of the erupting Vesuvius at Pompeii. He died in a cloud of poisonous fumes which no one could control.

THE BEAUTIFUL GAME?

11 May 2001

In 1966, when I became a curate in East Ham, I remember that Harry Redknapp was a young footballer at Upton Park. Every other Saturday I used to go with members of our youth club to watch the Hammers with their World Cup stars led by Bobby Moore. On Wednesday Harry Redknapp suffered the football manager's fate and left West Ham with his second in command, Frank Lampard. The papers profile Harry as being a manager who followed the West Ham principle that losing with style was preferable to winning without it, and far from thinking football was more important than life and death, he kept it firmly in proportion.

When I look back over those thirty-five years, it's easy to see how much football has changed: better stands and facilities, gigantic pay and transfer fees in a worldwide market. But is the game (there's a word which seems to be losing its meaning) in better health? We have seen supporters riot, tragic loss of life – again yesterday in Ghana, a panic followed by a stampede killed around one hundred and thirty people, sparked by a home loss and the measures taken for crowd control. In our own parks, referees are often subjected to abuse from players, who partly learn their lessons from the behaviour of professionals. Such great passions are aroused that they can become dangerous. Money and success become dominant in the running of the beautiful game.

Yet there is still so much to admire. The brilliant skills on show, the excitement of a good match, the exhilaration of victory, the sense of belonging, fans giving huge commitment, many travelling throughout Europe. The great rituals and choruses from men who would probably be horrified if asked to sing any hymn except 'Abide With Me'. The team strips seem a form of profiteering, but identifying with heroes is part of the thrill.

I sometimes think it wouldn't be a bad thing if we had a bit more of the passion, loyalty, participation and drama in church. But there is the root of the problem. If something you love becomes something you worship, treated as though it were God, it can become a total obsession and distort itself, becoming a substitute for important parts of life. So, long live football as a game, not just a business, and here's hoping Harry's creed can thrive in a new setting as it has at West Ham.

ENVIRONMENTAL
BILE DUCTS

18 May 2001

The arrival of our twin grandchildren over a year ago made a lot of changes in our lives. They provide a mixture of love, entertainment, wonder and tears. They've brought about one serious change in our thinking about the future. With our own children born in the sixties, we tended to think short term in our concerns about the world they would grow up in. Even though we knew knowledge and technology would advance at bewildering speed, we felt their world would be quite similar to ours. But as soon as we had grandchildren we started to think more long term. It's likely we will die before they are twenty and they will still have the main part of their lives ahead of them. So we ask more seriously what sort of world we shall leave them. When we see their future stretching long beyond our own, it makes us think more long term.

Almost every day we hear in the media about the possible results of our misuse of the earth, entrusted to us. Yesterday I read about an increase in liver cancer deaths – fifteen-fold in thirty years. It was the way the expert described the cause of the condition which struck me. He said that it was the result of being human in our own time. Because the liver is the sewage plant of the body, the bile ducts channel so many of the toxins which we encounter. It is there the tumour grows. Just another harmful result of our own behaviour as the human race.

Yet how are we ever to take the steps needed to protect our environment, our life on earth, when the market is god, when radical steps will not be taken because we only think short term or, as we heard earlier, the short horizon of our own economy, comfort and well-being? What will motivate us all and empower politicians to tackle the environmental bile ducts of human behaviour?

I've just been reading a book which makes the telling point that, although religion has often been the enemy of ecology, it could become a preserver. Religion has the power to motivate sacrificial action for a greater good. The Judaeo-Christian religions teach that the Lord saw his creation and it was good, and entrusted it to our stewardship. It will take powerful motivation to clean up our act and tackle these sins against our Creator.

JUDGEMENT – EARTHLY AND HEAVENLY

4 July 2001

The coincidence of the conviction of Barry George, the killer of Jill Dando, and the beginning of the trial of Slobodan Milošović, sharply raises a huge justice issue. The loner, Barry George, was unknown to most of us and the jury at his trial were not allowed to know about his previous conviction for rape, his history as a stalker of women and his earlier threat to Princess Diana. This was all kept hidden with the laudable aim that the verdict should not be based on a jury's prejudgement, but on evidence alone. Who can doubt that, with the widespread love of Jill Dando, the previous crimes would have made an impact on the judgement of us all, and probably the jury too.

On the other hand, the charges against Milošović are crimes against humanity. Well, we've all been hearing about them for years. Nothing can blot out all those TV pictures, the rows of bodies, the ethnic cleansing and the tragic wars between Serbia and her neighbours. It's hoped that the judges of the UN War Crimes Tribunal will, through international law, through their skill and objectivity, be able to tell the difference between evidence and prejudice.

This seems a long way short of the protection given to Barry George. But perhaps this is the price which has to be paid by those who have won power by constant appeal to the worst passions of the human race and who build their destructive regimes on injustice, terror and racial hate. This is the only way such dictators can be made accountable for their policies and the actions of their forces. It is to be hoped that the UN can, by justice in the tribunal, carry the trust of world opinion.

But there are always imperfections in the human justice system, whether at individual or international level; but for the sake of civilization, the search for justice has to go on.

One of the most testing facets of faith is the belief that we all live under the judgement of God. Sometimes I have feared it, but mostly, in the light of Christ, I have been thankful for its capacity to bring me back from what I regret. God's is a judgement where every part of our story is known, where we can trust the judge, where mercy and judgement meet, and above all where penitence can bring forgiveness and the chance to make reparation.

How Barry George and Milošović will fare before that judgement, God alone knows.

CONSCIENCE AND PROFIT

19 July 2001

In their report to Philip Morris, the world's biggest cigarette company, Arthur D. Little – consultants – advised that the Czech government saved between seventeen and twenty-one million pounds because smokers died years before their normal life expectancy. Even taking into account the cost of treating sick smokers, their government could make a total profit of over one hundred million pounds. The younger smokers pay tax on the habit, and when they're old the government saves on health care, pensions and housing, because of their premature death.

How do people on such boards of companies live with their decisions? Perhaps they believe self-harm is a right and, after all, everyone knows – even the young – that smoking can damage your health. Besides, I hear them say, 'It's not our job to make people's moral decisions for them; it's for government to set age limits and shopkeepers to observe them. In the end, it's down to each person and if they weren't able to smoke they'd die of stress; if we can't boost the sales to the Czechs, we could always expand the African market. Am I my brother's keeper?' If the argument was expressed in such crude terms what would a person of high moral intention do? Perhaps he'd say, 'Well, more people kill themselves with weapons or alcohol poisoning – it's not for industry to pontificate to people, young or old.' I've tried to imagine what I would do if I were an accountant on the board. I often think it's harder to be a Christian accountant than a Christian bishop – and I've been both. Whereas a bishop is expected to speak up for faith – that life is God-given and precious, that we are responsible for what we sell, that we should not try to persuade governments that it's profitable to shorten people's lives – a lay accountant has to struggle: 'How would the board react to anything so difficult as a religious belief? It's not my responsibility alone and my job's at stake; think of all the people we employ, think of the shareholders, think of the loss to the Treasury and the nation, think of the tobacco growers. It's all very well for the bishop, he has nothing to lose.'

But the problem is that Christ did teach that we are our brother's keeper. The only comfort I can think of for the board member is that we are all involved in actions which harm our universal brotherhood. In this country smokers pay ten billion pounds to the Treasury, but the fact that we are all involved is no excuse; it just makes us feel less alone.

DISINFECTING THE SPIRIT

25 July 2001

This week the pictures of farms being drenched with disinfectant to clean away any traces of foot and mouth disease made me ask how we can disinfect the human spirit. So many people have been infected by fear and dread of what might happen, or resentment and grief at what they have seen and experienced, livestock they have nurtured, shot and burnt on funeral pyres. All this wounded the spirit of farmers and, indeed, shocked and shamed the spirit of us all. But there's no material disinfectant which can cleanse the soul, appease the anger or remove the stain caused by this corporate tragic failure in management of the natural world.

I have seen real signs of hope – for instance, the Prince of Wales' call yesterday to government and society to tackle the countryside as a matter of urgency and ask for resources to rebuild what is so precious to us all. But we can't solve all our problems with money. Of course money is important, but we can't buy our way out of what goes on in our spirit. The disinfectant doesn't clear this infection, we can't go on tackling our rage with sedatives or identifying scapegoats. Because in our day we interpret what happens in such secular ways, we usually miss out on the divine assistance. Because we have let God be set aside, we lose our most precious source of hope when human management breaks down.

When South Africa became independent, Archbishop Desmond Tutu knew the people had to be cleansed of fear and hate, by facing the facts, facing each other, recognizing guilt and then, by prayer for reconciliation, bringing people towards trust in a genuine future.

I can't conceive of my life now without being drenched by the Spirit of God. There is, beyond ourselves, the Thou, the You, the otherness of God. When I think how often I take my failures, anger and bloody-minded selfishness to God, I wonder how I would hold together, how sustain cheerful hope, how find the energy to start again, if it were not by the cleansing, the fair judgement, the reparation God allows. As the psalmist prayed, 'Purge me with hyssop and I shall be clean, wash me and I shall be whiter than snow. Let me hear again your joy and gladness.'

I believe we need a public inquiry – not to point the finger of blame, but to learn and understand what has happened, in order to disinfect the human spirit and rebuild the trust and so enable the dialogue which is needed to plan together the future of farming and the countryside.

TWIN TOWERS

12 September 2001

I was sitting late last night in front of a blank piece of paper, my mind numbed by all we had seen, when a fax came in telling me that a daughter of two friends was missing in New York.

The pictures had seemed for a moment like an apocalypse or a brilliantly devised disaster movie, but now this was not myth or virtual reality, but life and death.

On a perfect morning in New York – which was looking impregnable – the vast twin towers were reduced to dust, and thousands on thousands of people were crushed in the fall. The Mayor of New York said the casualties would be more than any one of us can bear.

So many questions. Who did it? How would we all be affected? And rumbling from the ruins, the fear. This volcano didn't come from below but above, raining terror on Manhattan; not a natural disaster but man-made. What just cause could possibly deserve such an evil and unjust response? Will the appetite for retaliation lead to indiscriminate reprisals? Can even the good in the human mind cope wisely and effectively in the face of such evil? In this war no attempt was made to avoid civilian targets – indeed, somewhere over a long period people planned this blow precisely against innocent victims. As their bodies are recovered we are reminded that buildings can be replaced but lives cannot – they are beloved, and unique to those who love them.

This is man-made, but as a believer in God I still ask: what does God make of it? Perhaps the perpetrators believe in God. Some people even said this was a gift of God. Yet this denies everything that God means to me, and I know of no sane faith which would justify it.

And I asked God to say something I can say. 'Jesus wept' perhaps, or Christ's own words: 'My heart is ready to break with grief.' How God must grieve at the way we use the freedom he gives us. I know that even now prayer will be incessant in millions of minds – people waiting for news of a loved one, people already fearing reprisals, people so shocked and scared of what might happen, will turn to God, and maybe use old and familiar words to restore their courage and find confidence for the future: 'God is our hope and strength, a very present help in trouble, therefore will we not fear though the earth be moved.' The earth has moved. Please God help us.

WHOLESOME RELIGION

31 October 2001

In setting out his ethical justification for the action against terrorism in Afghanistan, the Prime Minister said yesterday: 'We are a principled nation and this is a principled conflict. We believe in our values of justice, tolerance and respect for all –

regardless of race, religion or creed.' Although the Christian influence was clearly there, he didn't promote it as from a Christian nation, but on principles he discerns in our multi-faith society. The terrorism was aimed at Muslims as it was against Christians and people of other faiths.

In the West, religion has to tackle secularization in a context in which faith is practised by minorities. This is so different from nations where Islam determines the identity and culture, where faith in Allah has often not been subjected to secular thinking. This is not a crusade, not a Christian-against-Muslim conflict.

As we have seen in the crosses on the coffins in Pakistan, the Jewish and Palestinian funerals in Israel, the years of Catholic and Protestant funerals in Northern Ireland, there are those who think 'a plague on all your houses' – the era of religion must come to an end – Road Closed. But, as we have seen in the equally barbaric atheist regimes, the religious thoughts, feelings and prayers of the people not only survive, but grow with more profound commitment.

If food is diseased we don't give up eating, but look for good, wholesome food; if water is polluted we don't stop drinking, but look for crystal-clear water. I believe that religion is a fundamental part of human nature, and we all worship in our way. It's as integral in our lives as our sexuality. Because there is so much prostituted sex, we don't give up yearning for love. Because religion can take hateful forms, can lure the disturbed into fanaticism, can deny the way of respect, tolerance and service which so much religion has in common – because we can pervert faith, it doesn't make it invalid, nor deny the reality of many people's encounter with God. Our secular society doesn't have all the answers – there are many stains on it. Christians have things to learn from true Islam, as Muslims have much from true Christian believing. Alongside the political, military and diplomatic initiatives, in the secular West we also need, in these terrible times, to discern our common ground and mobilize it.

DISPARAGEMENT – AN ART FORM

21 November 2001

This is my last 'Thought for the Day' as Bishop of Bath and Wells, because I retire in ten days' time. From now on my 'Thoughts' will be 'unofficial'.

Over the years I have kept on thinking how serious is our lack of respect for one another. We see it on the Tube, in the street, on television. I find this trend disturbing.

We've been having my farewell services in our cathedral at Wells with farmers, with teachers and schoolchildren. They've had a common theme – to give encouragement. As a nation we seem to have raised its opposite – disparagement – to an art form. Disparagement is defined as 'lowering of value, dishonour, discredit and indignity'. So many types of people experience this lowering of value. It's true of the farmers and teachers, but also of the police, doctors, nurses, even bishops; but above all, our politicians. For years the paper I read portrayed Mr Major daily in Y-front pants, Mr Hague as a bald dwarf and the Prime Minister as a maniac.

Of course we need pomposity punctured and hypocrisy exposed and then the lampoon may be justified, but is it any surprise that we have political apathy when politicians are persistently derided and lowered in honour?

One thing I've learnt about children – they thrive on encouragement and are vulnerable to disparagement. When I was a fat boy at school a teacher and my class mates debated whether I would survive longer if our ship sank in the Atlantic, because of my flab. That was an indignity I've never forgotten. But I also remember our chaplain saying to me: 'One day you'll go to university.' I eventually got there, partly because he believed in me. There's that lovely line about the oarsmen in Virgil's *Aeneid*:

'These men are nourished by success, they can do it because they think they can.'

Endless, pervasive disparagement is one of the causes of disrespect, which in turn is a root of violent and aggressive behaviour. It slowly erodes the dignity of people and undermines proper self-respect. As the praises to God echoed round the cathedral at those farewell services, I realized that receiving encouragement from God has been a huge factor in my life, defeating the lowering of value; I took strength from the fact that Jesus reached out and gave respect to people who were disparaged and so encouraged them to believe in God and believe in themselves.

A GOD WHO CAN WEEP

24 December 2001

It's lovely to do 'Thought for the Day' on Christmas Eve. The thoughts are nearly always linked to the news, and today Christ is the news. The Christian story is played out by children and adults in many schools and churches, and on Saturday I saw a brilliant version in a large marquee in which people of all ages from the community took part. It was not like the one I saw which became a producer's nightmare.

The trouble began because the baby Jesus was a doll which cried. When Mary picked it up, the baby cried . . . and cried . . . and cried. It was unstoppable. The wise men thought the baby should be removed. The shepherds favoured some sort of mechanical treatment, and the unseemly drama which ensued required a *Vicar of Dibley*-type intervention and the offending doll was carried out to the vestry to be 'pacified' – I think that was the word. But what looked like disaster restored the 'bite' to the story. Many of us were brought up on 'Away in a Manger':

> The cattle are lowing, the baby awakes,
> But little Lord Jesus no crying he makes.

These lines, intended to portray peaceful obedience, need a divine health warning. A baby who never cries would seem less than human. The birth of Christ identifies the wonder of God with the vulnerability of the baby – and with every human being – with your hurt and mine, as well as our joy.

For me this year, the hardest 'Thought' was on 12 September – to try to see some hope when our minds were numb. Then I came to those little words, 'Jesus wept.' God is not a remote, unfeeling landlord or tyrant, but immerses himself in the human agony as well as the ecstasy. Just as for many people this Christmas in Bethlehem will be a time of grief, worry and loneliness, so God has to be big enough, wide enough, high enough, deep enough, to be with us in our struggles. In the nativity of Christ – the much-needed sight of light and hope – with angels offering the promise of the peace we all long for, Christ is a refugee, fleeing from a child murderer, seeking asylum in Egypt. In all this human mess, God was giving himself for the world to bring goodwill, laughter and love. Only a God who can weep could do this thing.

THE QUEEN MOTHER
AND HISTORY

5 April 2002

Today we shall witness the Queen Mother's lying in state in the Great Hall at Westminster. As those brilliant BBC films showed last weekend, her gracious pilgrimage touched millions of our lives to the third and fourth generations, through wars and peace. Her lying in state is not just a tribute to a Queen, or to a great person, but also somehow a remembrance of the century itself – our national story which led us to the present day. I'm glad the parliaments of the United Kingdom gave space to reflect on her life and its times. If we forget our history we shall lose more than we have ever learnt.

This Easter week has been full of unresolved history – in the riots in Northern Ireland, an anniversary of the Falklands War, and, above all, the events in the Middle East stirring violence and fear in the familiar deadly cycle. The tanks drove into Bethlehem. The Church of the Nativity and Manger Square became commonplace names in a war zone, the City of David, the birthplace of Jesus, once more a battleground. The people on both sides of this conflict have a terror-filled history, and its horrors go on infecting the soul.

I vividly remember the first time I climbed down into the Grotto, where, according to ancient tradition, Christ was born. I experienced there the awesome mystery of God entering just such a time of unresolved history – with its own conflicts, occupied territory and refugees. He came as a baby, somehow to bring salvation. It is one of Christianity's most sacred places. When he became a man, he did not come by force of arms. He said, 'Those who live by the sword die by the sword.' He did not come riding a warhorse, but a donkey. He saw through the rage and spite to reveal to us, not a God of wrath and war, but of peace, truth, justice and mercy. 'My peace I give to you – not as the world gives' – a peace that comes through change of heart.

Last night we heard that President Bush had had a change of heart. 'Enough is enough.' Perhaps his intervention and General Colin Powell's journey will begin to face the history and be a real turning-point towards peace, not another mirage in the desert.

When we watch or even walk by the Queen Mother's coffin, we will no doubt say thank you for her life, and pray for her and her family. Perhaps at the same time we shall feel the weight of our history through those hundred and one years, and pray for a healing of history for the Israeli and Palestinian peoples.

AN ILL FOR EVERY PILL

13 April 2002

I always feel alert when people start talking about ageing, balding and weight problems – probably because I am ninety per cent bald, sixty-five per cent aged, and ten per cent over-weight. The *British Medical Journal* today is bravely pursuing the increasing tendency to treat facets of ordinary life, such as these, as disease. They call it 'the medicalization' of human experience. Being bald is a disappointment, being aged is unavoidable, and the ten per cent overweight could, in my case, be dealt with by an exercise of will – for none of these do I need medical treat-ment. Looking at American experience, the writers warn about 'A pill for every ill, and increasingly an illness for every pill.'

I call it 'brave' because defining disease crosses difficult boundaries which have often been fought over to get sufferers more help, to free them from stigma and lift the burden of responsibility. Distinctions do have to be made. Some people's overweight is an illness. But having sexual relationship problems is often not a disease; perhaps the two people need to have honest conversations, or recognize the causes of the fear of failure. Stress itself can cause illness, but there are many times when it too has to be seen as part of the package of daily life. There are those of us who ought to ring the doctor but don't, and others who ring the doctor but do not need to.

I believe this relates to the crisis in the NHS. I was struck by the Reith lecturer this week who was arguing that we concentrate so much on human rights, while ignoring human duties. In fact she suggested that if we don't attend to our human duty there can't be full human rights. The *BMJ* article warns us against medical dependency. It was religion that was called the opium of the people, whereas now we are heading towards drugs themselves being the opium.

Ironically, the Christian faith calls us to the duty of not misusing our body, which St Paul said is the 'temple of the Spirit' – that is good for us, good for others and good for the NHS. There's a lot of evidence that faith can provide the spirit to deal with the daily dis-ease of ordinary life. God offers medicine for the soul to tackle fear, anger and stress, to find forgiveness and bring love and hope. It's a free service. It gives the NHS more time to tackle the people who really need their care.

WOMEN'S WORK?

19 April 2002

As a recently appointed house husband, I was pleased to hear the Chancellor enthusiastically giving support to mothers in his Budget. I have a renewed sympathy for all the detailed tasks involved in running a home, and I'm not looking after children, or trying to do a job. Nor am I enduring a fight for survival.

The changing roles of men and women are a worldwide phenomenon, and the problems many women experience in the tension between a job and bringing up a family in the UK are part of that phenomenon..

A joint statement by UNICEF and UNESCO graphically describes the burden carried by women in the developing world:

> Women already grow most of its food, market most of its crops, fetch most of its water, collect most of the fuel, feed most of the animals, weed most of the fields. And when the work outside the house is done, they light the Third World's fires, cook its meals, clean its compounds, wash its clothes and look after its old and ill. All this as well as bearing and caring for the children.

This was written in 1993, and not a lot has changed. This life is so often a battle for survival, and the mothers are further bound by tradition and a religious inheritance which often reinforces male domination. Even when the men are unemployed, it would still be a matter for shame to do women's work. This requires education, not just for the women, but also for the men to see that real partnership can be enriching.

In this country, we have moved some way, but many pressures still remain. The mother can still be expected to do a job and retain all the other tasks. It can suit some men only too well.

Thankfully, more men now take their share in the domestic scene and don't see it as a threat, but an opportunity for a more tender and involved masculinity, a more just sharing of the responsibilities, and a greater opportunity to relate to the children and enjoy a more intimate marriage. In our hectic world, the demands of work on men as well as women need to take into account the importance of the home and having time for each other and the children. They will all be under stress if both spouses constantly arrive home exhausted, irritable and too tired for sympathy.

Religious ideas also have to change under God's Spirit and focus more on equality, partnership, bearing one another's burdens, and loving commitment to the family itself.

LE PEN

26 April 2002

This week I was moved to see thousands of young people protesting against Le Pen's reaching the second round in the French Presidential election. In the nation which coined the phrase '*Liberté, Egalité, Fraternité*', it was as though the young people woke out of sleep. They took responsibility and saw that this could become a threat against their civilization. Let's hope that those who did not vote will also be awake before the fifth of May. It's only too easy just to blame the politicians for such an aberration, but the electorate too are responsible for what happened.

We have no grounds for feeling superior. The General Election turnout here was extremely low and the local elections are forecast to dip below their already abysmally low response. Perhaps not voting is a protest against politics in general, but such a vacuum is dangerous and can give access to candidates whom the vast majority would reject, if they were awake to the danger. It took Hitler and his Nazis only eight years to come to power. One of his methods was to seduce the young into his Hitler Youth. The French people cannot have forgotten their own experience of the Nazis, let alone the six million people murdered in the cause of German racial purity. These were not only crimes against humanity, but a blasphemy. The roots of fascism are repellent to the understanding of the human race as Christ taught it and lived it. He reached out to the excluded, the different, the minorities, and revealed the potential and the value in every human being. He taught about what he called the Kingdom of God where justice reigns, where the Samaritan loved his neighbour, where the rich man tended to the needs of the poor man at his gate, and an African carried his cross.

The danger for us is the privatization of so much of our lives. We're so busy with our own agenda that we often delegate – abdicate perhaps – our duty, to the government, the charities, the Lottery. But change happens when people themselves commit time and energy to the needs of their community, refuse to become abstaining cynics, and take responsibility for their vote, and participate in democracy. It's been very hard won, and it can only be preserved by the young and the rest of us taking it seriously. The blasphemy of fascism has to be resisted by our citizens if Liberty, Equality, Fraternity are to be central to our civilization.